SURRENDERED GRACE

A 40-Day Lenten Journey of Renewal and Divine Direction

ELIORA HART

Copyright © 2026 by Eliora Hart

All rights reserved.

No part of this book may be reproduced, distributed, transmitted, stored in a retrieval system, or used in any form or by any means electronic, mechanical, photocopying, recording, scanning, or otherwise without the prior written permission of the publisher, except for brief quotations used in reviews or scholarly works.

Scripture quotations are taken from the Holy Bible, New International Version® (NIV®), New King James Version® (NKJV®), English Standard Version® (ESV®), and other translations. Scripture quotations are used with respect and for devotional purposes.

This book is a work of spiritual reflection and faith-based encouragement. Names, experiences, and examples are used illustratively to support devotional themes.

DISCLAIMER

This book is intended for **spiritual growth, reflection, and encouragement**. It is not intended to replace professional medical, psychological, pastoral, or legal advice. Readers are encouraged to seek qualified professionals for matters relating to mental health, physical health, or personal crises.

The prayers, reflections, fasting suggestions, and spiritual practices shared in this book are offered as **optional guides**, not obligations. Individual spiritual journeys vary, and readers should adapt practices according to personal health, spiritual maturity, and circumstances.

Fasting practices mentioned in this book should be approached with wisdom. If you have medical conditions, are pregnant, or have dietary restrictions, consult a healthcare professional before engaging in any form of fasting.

The author and publisher assume no responsibility for how the information in this book is used. All spiritual outcomes are deeply personal and dependent on individual engagement, prayer, and faith.

TABLE OF CONTENTS

- DISCLAIMER ... 3
- INTRODUCTION ... 10
  - What Is Lent? ... 10
- HOW TO USE THIS DEVOTIONAL ... 13
  - Entering the Journey with Intention ... 13
  - The Daily Structure of This Devotional ... 13
  - Scripture: Listening to the Living Word ... 14
  - Prayer: Responding with Honesty ... 14
  - Meditation: Learning to Be Still ... 15
  - Reflection: Examining the Heart ... 15
  - Application: Living What You Receive ... 16
  - Preparing Your Heart for the Journey ... 16
  - Surrendered Grace: Letting Go and Trusting God ... 16
  - A Word on Scripture Reading ... 17
  - Setting Expectations for Your 40-Day Journey ... 17
  - A Final Encouragement ... 18
- ASH WEDNESDAY TO THE WEEK OF SURRENDER ... 19
  - DAY 1 ... 20
  - A CALL TO SURRENDER ... 20
  - REFLECTION ... 20
  - MEDITATION ... 21
  - PRAYER ... 21
  - WORDS OF AFFIRMATION ... 22
  - ACTION STEP FOR TODAY ... 22
  - CLOSING REFLECTION ... 22
  - DAY 2: DUST AND GRACE ... 23
  - ACKNOWLEDGING HUMAN FRAILTY ... 23
  - DAY 3 ... 26
  - CONFESSION OF THE HEART ... 26
  - DAY 4 ... 29
  - FACING THE WILDERNESS WITHIN ... 29

DAY 5	32
SURRENDERING CONTROL	32
DAY 6	35
CHOOSING OBEDIENCE	35
DAY 7: REST DAY REFLECTION	38
SABBATH IN THE MIDDLE OF LENT	38
REPENTANCE & FORGIVENESS	**41**
DAY 8	42
TURNING FROM SIN	42
DAY 9	45
THE GIFT OF FORGIVENESS	45
DAY 10	48
GRACE THAT CLEANSES	48
DAY 11	51
RENEWAL OF THE MIND	51
DAY 12	54
REPAIRING BROKEN RELATIONSHIPS	54
DAY 13	57
EXTENDING FORGIVENESS TO OTHERS	57
DAY 14	60
THE FREEDOM OF FORGIVENESS	60
PRAYER AND CONTEMPLATION	**63**
DAY 15	64
SILENCE AND SOLITUDE	64
PRAYING WITHOUT CEASING	67
DAY 17	70
LISTENING FOR GOD'S VOICE	70
DAY 18	73
PETITION-ASKING, SEEKING, KNOCKING	73
DAY 19	76
GRATITUDE THROUGH THE STORM	76
DAY 20	79
ADORATION-WORSHIP IN TRUTH	79

DAY 21	82
THE PRACTICE OF WAITING	82
FASTING & SELF-DENIAL	**85**
DAY 22	86
WHAT ARE YOU HOLDING ON TO?	86
DAY 23	89
FAST FROM FEAR, FEAST ON FAITH	89
DAY 24	92
LETTING GO OF WORRY	92
DAY 25	95
FAST FROM JUDGMENT	95
DAY 26	98
CHOOSING PATIENCE	98
DAY 27	101
FAST FROM SELF-RELIANCE	101
DAY 28	104
FASTING WITH PURPOSE	104
SERVICE & COMPASSION	**107**
DAY 29	108
THE CALL TO SERVE	108
DAY 30	111
COMPASSION FOR THE HURTING	111
DAY 31	114
ALMS AND KINDNESS	114
DAY 32	117
SHARE YOUR STORY OF GRACE	117
DAY 33	120
SEEING CHRIST IN THE OTHER	120
DAY 34	123
THE EUCHARISTIC HEART-GIVE GENEROUSLY	123
DAY 35	126
REFLECTION-GRACE OVERFLOWING	126
SUFFERING, DEATH, AND HOPE	**129**

DAY 36	130
THE KING OF SURRENDER	130
DAY 37	133
SILENT OBEDIENCE	133
DAY 38	136
TRUTH IN THE FACE OF BETRAYAL	136
DAY 39	139
RENEWAL IN THE MIDST OF PAIN	139
DAY 40	142
LOVE BEYOND MEASURE	142
THE EMPTY TOMB RESURRECTION AND RENEWAL	145
Appendices	147
SCRIPTURE INDEX - 40 DAYS OF LENT	149
FINAL WORD	152
LIVING OUT SURRENDERED GRACE	152

HOW TO USE THIS BOOK

This devotional is designed to guide you gently and intentionally through **40 days of Lent**, from Ash Wednesday to Easter, helping you cultivate a life of **surrendered grace, spiritual resilience, and divine direction**.

1. Daily Structure

Each day includes:

- A **theme or focus** aligned with the Lenten journey
- **Scripture readings** to ground your reflection in God's Word
- A **devotional reflection** to guide your heart and mind
- **Reflection questions** for personal or group contemplation
- A **prayer** to help you respond to God
- **Words of affirmation** to reinforce spiritual truth

You may complete each day in **15–30 minutes**, or linger longer as the Spirit leads.

2. Pace Yourself

This book is meant to be read **one day at a time**, in order, following the rhythm of Lent. Avoid rushing. Lent is not about speed it is about **depth, honesty, and transformation**.

If you miss a day, do not be discouraged. Grace invites you to continue, not quit.

3. Engage Actively

For the richest experience:

- Keep a **journal** nearby
- Write your reflections honestly
- Sit in silence when prompted
- Pray aloud or quietly
- Revisit verses that stir your heart

Transformation happens when reflection becomes practice.

4. Use Individually or in Community

This book can be used:

- For **personal devotion**
- In **small groups or prayer circles**
- With **families or church study groups**

Reflection questions and prayers are suitable for group discussion and shared prayer.

5. Honor Your Health and Season

Fasting and self-denial are presented as **spiritual tools**, not rigid rules. You may fast from food, habits, distractions, fear, judgment, or anything the Spirit reveals. Choose what draws you **closer to God**, not what harms your body or spirit.

6. Carry the Lessons Beyond Lent

Though written for Lent, this book is meant to shape your life **beyond Easter**. Return to it whenever you need:

- Renewal
- Direction
- Healing
- A reminder of grace

Surrender is not seasonal it is a way of life.

Final Encouragement

Approach this book with an **open heart**, a **listening spirit**, and a willingness to be transformed. God meets surrendered hearts with abundant grace.

May this journey lead you not only to reflection but to resurrection living.

INTRODUCTION

What Is Lent?

Purpose, History & Meaning

Defining the 40-Day Journey of Grace (Biblical, Liturgical & Spiritual Roots)

Lent is one of the oldest and most profound seasons in the Christian liturgical calendar. At its core, it is a **40-day period of intentional spiritual preparation**, marked by prayer, reflection, repentance, fasting, and acts of love — all oriented toward the central mysteries of our faith: **the suffering, death, and resurrection of Jesus Christ**. This season invites believers into a deeper walk with God, a transformation of heart, and a renewed sense of divine direction.

1. The Origin and Purpose of Lent

Lent begins on **Ash Wednesday** and ends on **Holy Saturday**, the day before Easter Sunday. Traditionally observed in Western churches with a count of 40 days (excluding Sundays), it echoes Jesus's own **40 days of fasting and temptation in the wilderness** after His baptism (Matthew 4:1–11) — a time of testing, dependence on God, and preparation for ministry.

The number *40* carries deep biblical meaning as a period of **trial, purification, and transformation**, appearing throughout Scripture:

- **Moses** fasted for 40 days before receiving God's commandments (Exodus 34:28).
- **Elijah** journeyed 40 days to Mount Horeb (1 Kings 19:8).
- **The Israelites** wandered 40 years in the wilderness before entering the Promised Land.
- **Jesus** spent 40 days in spiritual confrontation and preparation.

By entering into this rhythm, believers symbolically walk with Christ into *the wilderness of surrender*, where distractions fall away and the soul refocuses on the things of God.

2. The Liturgical and Historical Roots

The word *Lent* comes from the Old English **lencten**, meaning *springtime* — a fitting metaphor for renewal and rebirth.
In the early centuries of the Church, Lent was closely tied to **preparation for baptism** at Easter. New believers (catechumens) underwent rigorous spiritual instruction, fasting, and prayer for 40 days leading up to their baptism at the Easter Vigil. Over time, this practice broadened to include all Christians, not just new converts.

By the **4th century**, the observance of Lent as a structured season before Easter was widely recognized in Christian communities. Councils such as **the Council of Nicaea (AD 325)** referenced this season of fasting and penitence, affirming its place in the rhythm of Church life.

Liturgically, Lent is traditionally a *penitential season* marked by themes of confession, introspection, and spiritual discipline preparing believers to enter Holy Week and approach Easter with reverence and gratitude.

3. The Spiritual Meaning of Lent

While Lent has formal and historical practices, its **deeper spiritual purpose** lies in its transformative invitation:

A Season of Repentance

Lent calls believers to "turn back" to God not out of guilt alone, but out of the recognition of **our need for divine mercy and grace**. The ashes imposed on Ash Wednesday symbolize our mortality, the brevity of life, and the need for heartfelt repentance.

A Time of Renewal

Just as spring nudges the natural world toward new life, Lent nudges the spiritual life of believers toward **renewal** a fresh start, a refined focus, a deeper awareness of God's presence.

A Journey of Grace

Ultimately, Lent isn't only about *giving things up* it's about **making space** for God to fill us with His presence. Whether through prayer, fasting, or acts of charity, the season invites us into a **renewed dependency on God's grace** and a heightened sensitivity to His leading.

4. The 40-Day Pathway of Grace

The shape of Lent mirrors Jesus's own spiritual journey. His wilderness experience was not merely an absence of food; it was a **deep encounter with God** — a time of spiritual strengthening before the ultimate act of sacrifice on the cross. Likewise, our Lenten journey becomes a **training ground for grace**, where disciplines of prayer, fasting, and generosity reorder the soul toward Christ.

This season prepares believers not only to remember Christ's death but to *participate in His life*, emerging into the joy of Easter with refreshed hearts, clearer vision, and renewed commitment to follow Him.

In this devotional, each of the 40 days will be an invitation to surrender more of what holds us back, to reflect more deeply on God's grace, and to seek His divine direction for the life ahead.

HOW TO USE THIS DEVOTIONAL

Entering the Journey with Intention

Lent is not meant to be rushed. It is not a challenge to complete, a box to check, or a spiritual performance to perfect. Lent is an invitation—an intentional slowing of the soul so that God may speak, heal, restore, and redirect. *Surrendered Grace* was designed as a companion for that sacred slowing, guiding you through forty days of intentional surrender, renewal, and divine direction.

This devotional is not about doing more for God, but about **making space for God to do more in you**. The structure, rhythms, and practices within these pages are meant to support—not burden your spiritual life. Whether you are new to Lent or returning with years of experience, this guide meets you where you are.

This chapter explains how to use the devotional effectively, how to prepare your heart, and what to expect as you walk through the forty-day journey.

The Daily Structure of This Devotional

Each day in *Surrendered Grace* follows a consistent, gentle rhythm. This repetition is intentional. Just as liturgy forms faith through familiar patterns, daily spiritual rhythms help anchor the soul.

Each day includes five core elements:

1. Scripture
2. Prayer
3. Meditation
4. Reflection
5. Application

You are encouraged to move through these elements slowly and prayerfully. Some days may resonate more deeply than others. That is normal. Trust that God is at work even when emotions or insights feel subtle.

Time Commitment

Most daily readings are designed to be completed in **15–25 minutes**. However, you are free to linger longer when the Spirit invites you to do so. Lent is not about efficiency—it is about attentiveness.

Scripture: Listening to the Living Word

Scripture is the foundation of each day's devotional. The Bible is not included merely for information, but for transformation. In Lent, Scripture becomes a mirror for the heart and a compass for the soul.

How to Read Scripture During Lent

- Read slowly, not hurriedly
- Read prayerfully, not analytically
- Read attentively, not defensively

You may find it helpful to read the passage **twice**:

- First, to hear the words
- Second, to listen for what God may be emphasizing

Do not worry if you do not understand every verse. Lent is not about mastering Scripture but about allowing Scripture to **master us**.

A Word of Encouragement

Some passages may confront you. Others may comfort you. Some may feel dry. All of them are gifts. Trust that God uses both clarity and mystery to shape the heart.

Prayer: Responding with Honesty

Prayer in this devotional is not scripted perfection—it is sacred honesty. Each prayer is offered as a guide, not a requirement. You are free to pray the words exactly as written or to use them as a starting point for your own conversation with God.

The Purpose of Prayer in Lent

Lenten prayer is not primarily about asking for blessings, though God welcomes our requests. It is about:

- Confession and repentance
- Surrender and trust
- Listening and waiting
- Alignment with God's will

Prayer during Lent reorients the heart from self-reliance to God-dependence.

Posture Matters

As you pray, consider your physical posture:

- Sitting quietly with open hands
- Kneeling in humility
- Standing in reverence

Your body often helps your soul enter prayer more fully.

Meditation: Learning to Be Still

Meditation in the Christian tradition is not emptying the mind, but **filling the heart with God's truth**. Each meditation invites you to sit with a word, phrase, or image from Scripture.

How to Practice Meditation

- Choose a quiet place
- Silence external distractions
- Breathe slowly and deeply
- Repeat a key phrase or truth
- Allow silence to do its work

At first, silence may feel uncomfortable. That discomfort often reveals how rarely we stop. Stay with it. God often speaks softly.

What Meditation Does

Meditation slows the soul, softens resistance, and opens space for God's grace. It trains us to listen rather than control.

Reflection: Examining the Heart

Reflection is where insight deepens and transformation begins. The reflection questions are designed to gently uncover areas where God may be inviting surrender, healing, or growth.

Be Honest, Not Impressive

There is no benefit in giving "correct" answers. God meets us in truth, not performance. If something feels uncomfortable, name it. If something feels confusing, admit it.

Journaling as a Spiritual Practice

If possible, keep a journal throughout Lent. Writing often reveals what the heart struggles to say aloud. Over time, you may notice patterns, prayers answered, or subtle shifts in perspective.

Application: Living What You Receive

Application connects prayer to daily life. Lent is not meant to remain abstract—it is meant to shape how we live, speak, love, and decide.

Applications may be:

- An action to take
- An attitude to release
- A habit to examine
- A relationship to heal

Do not underestimate small acts of obedience. Grace often works quietly.

Preparing Your Heart for the Journey

Before beginning Day One, take time to prepare your heart. Preparation matters because Lent is not merely a season on the calendar—it is a **posture of the soul**.

Create Sacred Space

Choose a consistent time and place for your devotional practice. Whether early morning or late evening, consistency creates expectation.

Release Pressure

You do not need to "feel spiritual" every day. God is faithful even when emotions fluctuate.

Set a Gentle Intention

Rather than setting rigid goals, set an intention such as:

- "I desire to listen more deeply."
- "I desire to trust God more fully."
- "I desire to surrender control."

Hold this intention lightly.

Surrendered Grace: Letting Go and Trusting God

The heart of this devotional is surrender—not resignation, but **trustful release**.

What Surrender Is Not

- It is not weakness
- It is not passivity
- It is not giving up hope

What Surrender Is

- An act of faith
- A posture of humility
- A declaration of trust

Grace meets us where control ends.

Why Surrender Matters

Many spiritual struggles come from trying to manage outcomes God never asked us to control. Lent invites us to loosen our grip and rediscover peace.

A Word on Scripture Reading

You may encounter familiar passages. Resist the urge to skim. Familiarity can dull attentiveness. Ask God to help you hear His Word with fresh ears.

If you miss a day, do not double back in guilt. Simply return. Grace does not keep score.

Setting Expectations for Your 40-Day Journey

Lent is not linear. Some days will feel rich. Others may feel empty. Trust that God works in both.

What You May Experience

- Increased self-awareness
- Emotional sensitivity
- Moments of clarity
- Resistance or discomfort
- Unexpected peace

All of these are signs of growth.

What This Journey Offers

Not perfection—but progress
Not answers—but alignment
Not control—but confidence in God

A Final Encouragement

As you begin *Surrendered Grace*, remember this:
God is more committed to your transformation than you are.

Come as you are. Stay open. Let grace lead.

This is not just forty days of reading, it is forty days of **becoming**.

WEEK 1

ASH WEDNESDAY TO THE WEEK OF SURRENDER

Theme: Letting Go for Renewal

The opening week of Lent sets the spiritual tone for the entire journey. Beginning on **Ash Wednesday**, this week invites us to pause, humble ourselves, and acknowledge our deep need for God. The ashes remind us of our mortality and our dependence on divine grace, calling us to release pride, self-reliance, and distractions that cloud our hearts.

This week focuses on **letting go**—not as loss, but as a sacred exchange. As we surrender control, old habits, fears, and misplaced priorities, we create space for spiritual renewal. Letting go allows God to re-center our lives, soften hardened areas of the heart, and restore clarity where confusion has taken root.

Throughout this week, you are encouraged to approach surrender gently and honestly. Renewal begins when we stop striving and start trusting, recognizing that true transformation flows not from our effort, but from God's grace working within us. This first step of surrender lays the foundation for the deeper work God will continue throughout the remaining days of Lent.

DAY 1

A CALL TO SURRENDER

Scripture:

"Return to the Lord your God, for He is gracious and merciful, slow to anger, and abounding in steadfast love…" — **Joel 2:13 (ESV)**

Ash Wednesday marks the **beginning of the Lenten journey** a season of prayer, fasting, repentance, and renewal. The word *Lent* simply means a period of preparation. On this day, Christians around the world step into a sacred rhythm that echoes the words of Scripture: *"Repent, and believe in the Gospel."* It is both solemn and hopeful a moment to reflect on our brokenness and yet open our hearts to God's abundant grace.

Ash Wednesday takes its name from the ancient practice of placing **ashes on the forehead in the shape of a cross** a visible reminder of mortality and a symbolic invitation to turn away from sin and toward God. The tradition connects us to the biblical symbolism of ashes in Scripture, which often express **penitence, humility, and mourning for sin** (e.g., Daniel 9:3; Jonah 3:6).

Introduction to the Theme: A Call to Surrender

Today's theme is **surrender** not a weak giving up, but a strong *letting go* of our self-will, pride, and self-reliance so that God can shape our hearts. Where we cling to control, God invites us to trust. Where we hold tightly to comfort, He calls us to release. Where we bury sin in silence, God beckons us to repent honestly.

Ash Wednesday challenges us to examine our hearts deeply. It asks:

- What have we held onto that keeps us from God?
- Where have we placed our confidence instead of in Christ?
- In what ways have we tried to navigate life apart from God's direction?

This day begins with confession a turning toward God with all our hearts because God *is gracious, merciful, and slow to anger* (Joel 2:13).

REFLECTION

Ash Wednesday opens with a sober truth: *"Remember that you are dust, and to dust you shall return."* (Genesis 3:19) a phrase often spoken as ashes are imposed on the forehead. This reminder of mortality isn't meant to discourage us; rather, it grounds us in reality and invites us to live with eternal perspective.

Our mortality teaches us several key spiritual truths:

1. **Life is fragile** — and every moment is a gift.
2. **Sin has real consequences**, but grace has greater power.
3. **Our pursuit of worldly things pales** compared to pursuing Christ.

Ashes remind us that we are created beings dependent on God for every breath. But they also reflect the beautiful paradox of the Gospel: **from dust, God forms life; through death, Christ brings life; and in surrender, God pours out grace.**

Lent begins not with strength, but humility. It begins not with pride, but confession. It begins not with control, but surrender.

MEDITATION

Take a quiet moment to breathe slowly and reflect on these words:

"Return to the Lord your God..." (Joel 2:13)

Let them settle into your heart with each breath.

Ask yourself:

- **What does it mean for me to *return* to God today?**
- **What in my life needs to be surrendered so that God can renew me?**

Sit in silence before the Lord. Allow His presence to remind you that surrender is not defeat — it is the beginning of freedom.

PRAYER

Heavenly Father,
On this first day of Lent, I come before You with a humble heart. I acknowledge my limitations, my failures, and my need for Your mercy. Today I lay down my pride, my misplaced confidence, and all that separates me from You.

Teach me to surrender not reluctantly, but joyfully knowing that Your grace meets me where I am and calls me higher. Help me to turn back to You fully, to trust You deeply, and to follow You faithfully.

Forgive me where I have strayed. Renew my heart, O Lord, and make me new in Your steadfast love. Let this season of Lent draw me closer to You, and prepare me for the joy of resurrection at Easter.
In Jesus' name, Amen.

WORDS OF AFFIRMATION

Speak these truths aloud and let them shape your soul today:

- **I am beloved by God, and He meets me in my humility.**
- **Today, I surrender what I cannot control, and trust God with what I can't see.**
- **I seek God's mercy with an honest and open heart.**
- **Ashes remind me of my limitations but God reminds me of His limitless grace.**

May these affirmations anchor you as you begin this Lenten journey.

ACTION STEP FOR TODAY

Pause and Surrender

As you go about your day, take intentional moments to surrender something specific — whether a worry, a fear, or a desire for control. Consciously release it to God in prayer, saying:

"Lord, I surrender this to You."

Consider also incorporating a simple act of fasting, prayer, or almsgiving a tangible reminder that your dependence is on God alone.

CLOSING REFLECTION

Ash Wednesday reminds us that the spiritual journey of Lent begins with honesty honesty about who we are, our mortality, and our need for God. As we surrender our hearts today, we set the foundation for deeper renewal in the days ahead.

Lent is not about earning God's love. It is about **receiving His mercy more fully** and turning more deeply toward His presence. May this day of ashes be for you a sacred beginning a call to surrender, a call to trust, and a call to grace.

DAY 2: DUST AND GRACE

ACKNOWLEDGING HUMAN FRAILTY

Scripture Reading:

"Then the Lord God formed man from the dust of the ground and breathed into his nostrils the breath of life, and the man became a living being." — **Genesis 2:7 (NRSV)**

"As for mortals, their days are like grass; they flourish like a flower of the field; for the wind passes over it, and it is gone... But the steadfast love of the Lord is from everlasting to everlasting." — **Psalm 103:15–17 (NRSV)**

Introduction: Formed from Dust, Sustained by Grace

On this second day of Lent, we remain close to the ashes of Ash Wednesday—but we begin to see them more clearly. Yesterday, the ashes reminded us of our mortality. Today, they teach us something deeper: **human frailty is not a flaw—it is the place where grace begins**.

Scripture tells us that humanity was formed from dust. This is not a statement of insignificance, but of **origin and dependence**. We are not self-made. We are not self-sustaining. Every breath we take is borrowed from God's generosity. To acknowledge our frailty is not to diminish our worth—it is to remember our true relationship with the Creator.

Lent gently dismantles the illusion of self-sufficiency. In a world that celebrates strength, productivity, and control, this season invites us to confess a quieter truth: *we are fragile, limited, and deeply in need of God*. And yet—astonishingly—we are also deeply loved.

This is where dust meets grace.

Reflection: The Gift of Remembering Our Limits

To be human is to live within limits. Our bodies tire. Our emotions fluctuate. Our plans fail. Our wisdom is incomplete. Yet so much of our striving comes from trying to deny these realities.

Ashes remind us that:

- We cannot control time
- We cannot escape weakness
- We cannot sustain ourselves

But grace reminds us that:

- God holds our time
- God meets us in weakness
- God sustains what we cannot

Psalm 103 paints a vivid contrast: our lives are like grass—brief and vulnerable—*but* God's love is everlasting. Lent is not meant to leave us dwelling in our frailty alone; it leads us to see how **God's mercy surrounds our fragility.**

Acknowledging human frailty frees us from pretending. It allows us to stop proving, striving, and hiding. When we admit our dustiness, we open ourselves to God's breath—the same breath that turned dust into life.

Ask yourself today:

- Where am I exhausted from trying to be strong?
- What weakness have I been resisting instead of surrendering?
- How might God be inviting me to rest in His sufficiency?

Meditation: Held Between Dust and Breath

Find a quiet place. Sit comfortably. Place one hand over your heart and the other open on your lap.

Breathe in slowly and silently pray:
"You formed me."

Breathe out slowly and pray:
"You sustain me."

Repeat this several times.

As you breathe, imagine God's breath filling what feels empty, tired, or fragile within you. Remember: the same God who formed you from dust continues to breathe grace into your life today.

A Word on Grace

Grace is not given because we are strong.
Grace is given because we are not.

The Gospel does not begin with human capability—it begins with divine compassion. Jesus entered fully into human frailty: hunger, fatigue, sorrow, suffering, even death. He did not bypass weakness; He redeemed it.

Lent teaches us that grace does not remove our limits—it **meets us within them**.

Prayer

Gracious God,
Today I remember that I am dust—formed by Your hands and sustained by Your breath. I confess how often I forget my dependence on You, striving to be strong on my own and hiding my weakness from You and others.

Teach me to accept my frailty without shame and to trust Your grace without fear. Where I feel limited, remind me that You are limitless. Where I feel weak, remind me that Your strength is made perfect in weakness.

Breathe new life into me today. Hold me gently as I learn to rest in You.
In Jesus' name, Amen.

Words of Affirmation

Speak these words slowly and intentionally:

- **I am created by God and sustained by His grace.**
- **My weakness does not disqualify me—it draws me closer to God.**
- **I release the burden of self-sufficiency and rest in God's care.**
- **Though I am dust, I am deeply loved.**

Let these truths shape how you see yourself today.

Application: Practicing Humble Dependence

Today, practice one simple act of humility:

- Ask for help instead of pushing through alone
- Take a moment of rest without guilt
- Offer a silent prayer before a routine task
- Admit a limitation without self-criticism

Let this act remind you that dependence on God is not failure—it is faith.

Closing Reflection

Lent invites us to live honestly acknowledging both our fragility and God's faithfulness. We are dust, yes but dust held in the hands of a gracious Creator.

DAY 3

CONFESSION OF THE HEART

Scripture Reading:

"If we confess our sins, He who is faithful and just will forgive us our sins and cleanse us from all unrighteousness." — **1 John 1:9 (NRSV)**

"Create in me a clean heart, O God, and put a new and right spirit within me." — **Psalm 51:10 (NRSV)**

Introduction: Returning with an Honest Heart

Confession is one of the most misunderstood spiritual practices. Many associate it with shame, punishment, or fear of exposure. Yet in Scripture, confession is consistently portrayed as an act of **freedom**, not condemnation. It is not a moment where God turns away from us—but where we finally turn toward God.

On this third day of Lent, we are invited into the **confession of the heart**—a gentle but courageous practice of honesty before God. Confession is not merely listing wrong actions; it is allowing God to search our motives, our desires, our fears, and our hidden places. It is the surrender of the inner life.

Lent creates sacred space for this kind of truth-telling. In a culture that encourages denial and self-justification, confession becomes a countercultural act of trust. We confess not because God is harsh, but because **God is faithful and just**, eager to forgive and restore.

Reflection: Truth That Heals

Psalm 51 was written by King David after being confronted with his sin. Rather than hiding or defending himself, David opens his heart fully before God. His prayer reveals something essential about confession: **God desires truth in the inward being** (Psalm 51:6).

Confession does three important things:

1. **It names reality** — breaking the power of denial
2. **It restores relationship** — removing barriers between us and God
3. **It renews the heart** — making space for grace and healing

Unconfessed sin does not disappear—it quietly shapes us. It hardens the heart, clouds spiritual clarity, and weakens intimacy with God. Confession, by contrast, brings what is hidden into the light, where grace can do its work.

Ask yourself today:

- What have I been avoiding bringing before God?
- Where do I feel distant, defensive, or spiritually numb?
- What would it look like to trust God fully with the truth of my heart?

Remember: God already knows. Confession is not about informing God—it is about **aligning ourselves with truth**.

Meditation: Sitting in God's Light

Find a quiet place. Close your eyes. Take a slow breath.

Silently pray:
"Search me, O God, and know my heart." (Psalm 139:23)

Imagine yourself standing in gentle light—not harsh or exposing, but warm and welcoming. Allow God to reveal anything that needs healing, release, or forgiveness.

Do not rush. Do not judge yourself. Simply notice what arises and place it before God with trust.

A Word on Repentance

Confession leads naturally to repentance. Repentance is not self-condemnation—it is **reorientation**. It means turning away from what diminishes life and turning toward what restores it.

True repentance always carries hope, because it is rooted in God's mercy, not our effort.

Prayer

Merciful God,
I come before You with an open heart. I confess that I have sinned—not only in my actions, but in my thoughts, attitudes, and desires. I have held onto pride, fear, resentment, and distraction. I have trusted myself more than I have trusted You.

Yet I thank You that You are faithful and just to forgive. Cleanse my heart, O God. Create in me a new spirit. Restore what has been broken and renew what has grown weary.

Help me to walk in truth, freedom, and humility. Teach me to live honestly before You, trusting in Your mercy every day.
In Jesus' name, Amen.

Words of Affirmation

Speak these words slowly and with faith:

- **I am forgiven through the grace of God.**
- **Confession leads me into freedom, not shame.**
- **God renews my heart as I walk in truth.**
- **I am cleansed, restored, and made new in Christ.**

Let these affirmations remind you of God's faithful love today.

Application: Practicing Confession Today

Choose one intentional practice today:

- Write a private prayer of confession in your journal
- Spend a few moments in silent repentance
- Release a burden you've been carrying into God's care
- Seek reconciliation where God prompts you

Confession is not a one-time act—it is a way of living honestly before God.

Closing Reflection

Confession opens the door to renewal. When we bring the truth of our hearts before God, we discover that mercy is already waiting.

Lent reminds us that we are not called to hide we are called to return. And every return is met with grace.

DAY 4

FACING THE WILDERNESS WITHIN

Scripture Reading:

"Then Jesus was led up by the Spirit into the wilderness to be tempted by the devil. He fasted forty days and forty nights, and afterwards he was famished." — **Matthew 4:1–2 (NRSV)**

"He said to me, 'My grace is sufficient for you, for my power is made perfect in weakness.' Therefore I will boast all the more gladly of my weaknesses, so that the power of Christ may dwell in me." — **2 Corinthians 12:9 (NRSV)**

Introduction: Entering the Inner Wilderness

On the fourth day of Lent, we are invited to face the **wilderness within**—the inner terrain where fears, doubts, unresolved wounds, and unexamined habits reside. Just as Jesus was led into the physical wilderness, each of us has an internal landscape that calls for honesty, courage, and surrender.

The wilderness can be uncomfortable. It is often a place of silence, emptiness, or confrontation with what we would rather ignore. Yet it is also a **place of preparation**, growth, and transformation. The same Spirit that led Jesus into the desert is present to guide us through our own inner landscapes, helping us confront the shadows, release control, and experience God's sustaining presence.

Facing the wilderness is not about punishment—it is about **discovery and renewal**. Within the starkness of our internal deserts, we meet God in ways that are deep, raw, and life-giving.

Reflection: Recognizing the Wild Places

The wilderness within takes many forms:

- Persistent fears or anxieties that control your decisions
- Resentments and unforgiveness toward yourself or others
- Habits or patterns that leave you spiritually depleted
- Doubts about God's plan or your purpose

Ask yourself:

- What areas of my life feel barren, dry, or empty?
- Where am I resisting God's shaping hand because it feels uncomfortable?
  - How might God be inviting me to encounter Him even in this wilderness?

The desert may feel lonely, but it is also **fertile soil for transformation**. God often speaks most clearly in places where our control ends and our dependence begins.

2 Corinthians 12 reminds us that weakness is not failure. Our vulnerabilities, struggles, and limitations are **opportunities for God's power and grace to dwell** more fully in our lives.

Meditation: Sitting in the Desert

Take a quiet moment to breathe deeply. Imagine yourself standing in an open, barren landscape. The ground is dry, and the wind moves across the sand. Yet in the distance, there is light—steady, constant, inviting.

Focus on this phrase from Scripture:
"My grace is sufficient for you." (2 Corinthians 12:9)

Allow your heart to name areas of fear, doubt, or resistance. Offer each one silently to God, trusting that His grace is enough to sustain you even in the wilderness.

Prayer

Loving God,
Today I bring before You the deserts of my heart. I confess the fears, doubts, and struggles I often try to hide. I admit my need for Your presence, guidance, and strength.

Walk with me through this wilderness. Teach me to see Your light where I see emptiness. Teach me to feel Your strength where I feel weakness. Help me to surrender the need to control and trust in Your perfect timing and abundant provision.

Let this season of Lent be a time where I am renewed, even in the dry and barren places of my soul.
In Jesus' name, Amen.

Words of Affirmation

Speak these truths aloud to reinforce your faith:

- **God's grace is sufficient for me, even in my weakness.**
- **The wilderness I face is fertile ground for growth.**
- **I surrender my fears and doubts to God's loving care.**
- **Even in emptiness, I am held, guided, and renewed.**

Application: Embracing the Wilderness

Choose one intentional action today:

- Identify one area of your life that feels barren or challenging. Pray specifically for God's guidance there.
- Practice silence for 10–15 minutes, acknowledging feelings or thoughts you usually avoid.
- Write down one fear or limiting belief and consciously release it into God's hands.

Remember: the wilderness is not a place of defeat—it is a classroom where God teaches resilience, trust, and transformation.

Closing Reflection

The wilderness within may be uncomfortable, but it is necessary. Just as Jesus emerged from the desert ready for ministry, we too emerge from our inner wilderness strengthened, sharpened, and open to God's leading.

Facing the wilderness is an act of courage and faith. Today, embrace the desert, knowing that grace meets you there. Surrender, trust, and walk forward with confidence that God is shaping something beautiful in your life even in the dry places.

DAY 5

SURRENDERING CONTROL

Scripture Reading:

"Trust in the Lord with all your heart, and do not rely on your own insight. In all your ways acknowledge him, and he will make straight your paths." — **Proverbs 3:5–6 (NRSV)**

"Cast all your anxiety on him, because he cares for you." — **1 Peter 5:7 (NRSV)**

Introduction: Letting Go to Let God Work

As we enter the fifth day of our Lenten journey, we confront a core struggle of the human heart: **the desire to control outcomes, circumstances, and even the actions of others**. While control can feel like safety, it often leads to stress, disappointment, and distance from God.

Today's theme is **surrendering control** a conscious decision to release our grip on life and entrust it fully to God. Surrender does not mean passivity; it means **choosing to cooperate with God's will rather than forcing our own agendas**. It is an act of trust, humility, and courage.

Lent invites us to practice this daily. Each time we let go of control, we make space for God's grace to flow into situations we cannot fix or understand. By releasing what we cannot manage, we align ourselves with divine wisdom and experience peace that surpasses human understanding.

Reflection: The Illusion of Control

Control is seductive. We often believe that if we can manage everything—our schedules, outcomes, relationships—we will be safe, happy, or secure. Yet Scripture repeatedly reminds us that **our insight is limited**, and true life is found in dependence on God (Proverbs 3:5–6).

Reflect on these questions today:

- What areas of my life am I clinging to too tightly?
- Where am I trying to manipulate outcomes instead of trusting God's timing?
- What fears or anxieties arise when I consider letting go?

1 Peter 5:7 reminds us that surrender is also a relief: *"Cast all your anxiety on Him."* Anxiety often grows in proportion to our attempts to control what is not ours to manage. Surrender, therefore, is a path to freedom.

Consider surrender as a **daily discipline**—not a single moment of release, but a continual choice to trust God more than your own understanding.

Meditation: Resting in God's Hands

Find a quiet space. Place your hands palm-up as if offering your life to God. Close your eyes and repeat these phrases slowly, letting each sink into your heart:

- *Lord, I surrender this moment.*
- *I release my plans and my fears into Your care.*
- *Your will, not mine, be done.*

Visualize yourself handing over worries, deadlines, or burdens. Imagine them resting gently in God's hands, being held with infinite wisdom, care, and love.

Prayer

Faithful God,
I confess how often I cling to control—over my day, my relationships, and even the outcomes of my life. I admit that this striving leaves me anxious and weary. Today, I surrender my need to manage everything.

Help me trust You more fully. Teach me to release fears, worries, and expectations into Your care. Show me how to walk in obedience and peace, knowing that You are guiding my steps, even when I cannot see the path ahead.

Thank You for holding what I cannot, and for shaping my life with wisdom and love. Let this Lenten season be a practice of surrender that deepens my faith and draws me closer to You. In Jesus' name, Amen.

Words of Affirmation

Say these truths aloud as a declaration of faith:

- **I release control and trust God's perfect plan.**
- **God's grace sustains me even when I cannot manage life.**
- **Surrender is freedom, not weakness.**
- **I place my anxieties, plans, and desires in God's loving hands.**

Let these affirmations guide your heart throughout the day.

Application: Practical Steps to Surrender

Today, take one intentional action to practice surrender:

- Identify one decision or worry you have been trying to control. Pray over it and consciously release it to God.
- Take a short walk or pause during the day to reflect: *"I trust God with this moment."*
- Let go of perfectionism in a task today and accept God's strength to guide the outcome.
- Offer grace to someone else, acknowledging that you cannot control their actions.

Remember, surrender is a practice—not a one-time act. Each small release strengthens your trust in God.

Closing Reflection

Control is an illusion; grace is real. As you surrender today, notice the freedom and peace that begin to replace anxiety and striving. Trusting God does not mean life becomes easy—but it does mean you no longer carry what is not yours to bear.

Surrender is the soil where faith grows. Today, commit to letting go, trusting God, and walking forward in peace.

DAY 6

CHOOSING OBEDIENCE

Scripture Reading:

"If you love me, you will keep my commandments." — **John 14:15 (NRSV)**

"But be doers of the word, and not merely hearers who deceive themselves." — **James 1:22 (NRSV)**

Obedience as an Act of Love

As we approach the end of the first week of Lent, today's focus shifts from surrendering control to **choosing obedience**. Obedience is often misunderstood as restriction or burden, yet Scripture presents it as a **loving response to God's grace**. We obey not to earn God's favor, but because we already belong to Him.

In Lent, obedience becomes deeply personal. It is not about rigid rule-keeping, but about aligning our lives—our decisions, habits, and attitudes—with God's will. When we choose obedience, we are choosing trust over fear, faith over convenience, and relationship over independence.

Jesus links obedience directly to love. Obedience flows naturally from a heart that trusts God's goodness and desires to walk in His ways.

Reflection: Hearing and Doing

James warns us that it is possible to hear God's Word without allowing it to shape our lives. Lent invites us beyond spiritual awareness into **spiritual action**.

Obedience often appears in small, quiet choices:

- Speaking truth when silence feels safer
- Practicing patience instead of reacting
- Forgiving when resentment feels justified
- Saying "yes" to God when it costs comfort

Ask yourself:

- Where might God be inviting me to take a step of obedience today?
- What fears or excuses keep me from responding fully?
- How does obedience deepen my relationship with God?

Obedience is rarely dramatic. More often, it is faithful consistency—choosing God again and again in ordinary moments.

MEDITATION: ALIGNING THE WILL

Sit quietly and breathe slowly. With each breath, repeat this simple prayer:

"Lord, align my will with Yours."

As you breathe, imagine your desires gently yielding to God's wisdom. Ask God to reveal one specific area where obedience is needed—not out of pressure, but out of love.

Remain still for a few moments, listening.

A Word on Freedom

True obedience leads to freedom. When we live according to God's truth, we are released from the bondage of fear, guilt, and self-centered living. God's commands are not chains—they are pathways to life.

Prayer

Faithful and Loving God,
I thank You for Your Word, which guides and shapes my life. I confess that there are times I hear Your voice but hesitate to respond. Fear, comfort, and distraction often pull me away from obedience.

Today, I choose to follow You. Strengthen my heart to respond with trust and humility. Teach me to obey not out of obligation, but out of love. Help me to walk in Your ways and reflect Your truth in my daily life.

Let my obedience be a witness of Your grace at work within me.
In Jesus' name, Amen.

Words of Affirmation

Speak these truths aloud:

- **I choose obedience as an expression of my love for God.**
- **God's Word guides my steps and shapes my life.**
- **Through obedience, I grow in faith and freedom.**
- **I trust God's wisdom above my own understanding.**

Application: Practicing Obedience Today

Today, intentionally act on one prompting from God:

- Obey a clear instruction from Scripture
- Respond kindly where you might normally withdraw
- Take a step of faith you've been delaying
- Release a habit or behavior God has been asking you to change

Let obedience today be simple, sincere, and faith-filled.

Closing Reflection

Choosing obedience is choosing life. It is saying "yes" to God's guidance, even when the path feels uncertain. As this first week of Lent draws to a close, remember that obedience deepens trust and prepares your heart for continued renewal.

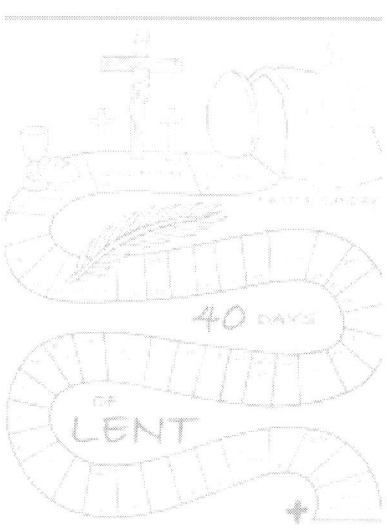

DAY 7: REST DAY REFLECTION

SABBATH IN THE MIDDLE OF LENT

Scripture Reading:

"Remember the sabbath day, and keep it holy. Six days you shall labor and do all your work. But the seventh day is a sabbath to the Lord your God..." — **Exodus 20:8–10 (NRSV)**

"Come to me, all you that are weary and are carrying heavy burdens, and I will give you rest." — **Matthew 11:28 (NRSV)**

Embracing Rest in the Midst of Discipline

After six days of reflection, surrender, and discipline, Lent calls us to pause: to **rest, reflect, and receive**. Today is a Sabbath day a gift in the middle of the journey to allow our hearts and spirits to catch up with the work of God already begun.

Lent is not about relentless striving; it is about **transformation through rhythm**. Just as God rested after creation, we too are invited to embrace a day of spiritual rest. Sabbath is not laziness it is **holy restoration**, a chance to realign with God's presence and renew our souls.

In the first week of Lent, we have faced ashes, acknowledged our frailty, confessed our sins, explored the wilderness of the heart, surrendered control, and chosen obedience. Today, Sabbath gives space to **absorb these lessons, deepen reflection, and allow God's grace to settle within us**.

Reflection: The Gift of Sabbath

Sabbath reminds us that **we are not defined by our productivity, achievements, or self-effort**, but by God's love and care. When we rest, we declare:

- Life is not solely about doing; it is about being.
- God's work in us is ongoing, even when we pause.
- Peace and renewal are found in presence, not performance.

Reflect on these questions:

- How often do I allow myself to truly rest before God?
- What burdens have I been carrying that need to be released today?
- How can Sabbath help me embrace God's rhythm of grace during Lent?

Rest is an act of trust: trusting that God's grace continues even when we stop striving.

Meditation: Being Still in God's Presence

Find a quiet space and sit comfortably. Place your hands open on your lap. Close your eyes and breathe deeply.

As you breathe in, say: *"Lord, I come to You."*
As you breathe out, say: *"I release my burdens."*

Visualize placing each worry, fear, and unfinished task at God's feet. Imagine His presence surrounding and renewing you. Stay in silence, listening, resting, and receiving His love.

A Word on Rest

Sabbath is not just physical rest—it is **spiritual restoration**. It reminds us that God's care is not contingent on our activity. By practicing Sabbath during Lent, we learn that obedience and discipline are balanced by mercy and rest.

Jesus' invitation in Matthew 11:28–30 is central: *"Come to me... and I will give you rest."* Lent is a time to embrace both discipline and divine rest, allowing God to strengthen our hearts for the journey ahead.

Prayer

Gracious God,
Today I pause in Your presence. I lay down the burdens I have been carrying—my worries, my striving, my attempts to control. I accept Your invitation to rest.

Help me embrace Sabbath as sacred time to be renewed and restored. Teach me to trust Your timing, to delight in Your presence, and to receive Your peace. May this day of rest prepare my heart for the challenges and joys of the days to come.

Thank You for Your unending grace and for walking with me even when I pause.
In Jesus' name, Amen.

Words of Affirmation

Speak these aloud, letting them sink into your spirit:

- **I am held and renewed by God's presence.**
- **Rest is holy, and I embrace it without guilt.**
- **God's grace continues even when I pause.**
- **Today I receive peace and restoration for my soul.**

Application: Practicing Sabbath Today

- Take a deliberate break from work or responsibilities, even if brief.
- Engage in a restful activity that draws you closer to God—reading Scripture, praying, or sitting in silence.
- Reflect on the lessons from the past six days of Lent, journaling any insights.
- Release control over outcomes today, trusting God to work even when you rest.

Sabbath is a gift. Use it to nourish your soul and deepen your trust in God.

Closing Reflection

Rest is not passive—it is active trust. By embracing Sabbath in the middle of Lent, we affirm that **our worth is found in God's love, not our effort**, and that renewal comes when we pause, reflect, and receive His grace.

WEEK 2

REPENTANCE & FORGIVENESS

Theme: Turning Back to God
Scripture Focus: *"Repentance transforms the heart"*

The second week of Lent guides us deeper into the spiritual disciplines of **repentance and forgiveness**. While the first week focused on surrendering control and beginning the journey of renewal, this week emphasizes **turning back to God** with honest hearts. Repentance is more than acknowledging sin—it is an active **realignment of our lives with God's will**, allowing His grace to reshape our desires, choices, and priorities.

Forgiveness, both received and extended, accompanies repentance. As we confront our failures, we are reminded that God's mercy is greater than our mistakes, and that we are called to reflect that mercy to others. By embracing repentance, we experience transformation: bitterness is replaced with peace, guilt with freedom, and pride with humility.

Throughout this week, Scripture anchors us in the truth that **repentance transforms the heart**. Each reflection, prayer, and act of forgiveness becomes a step closer to the God who heals, restores, and renews. This is a week of **turning inward and upward**, surrendering past mistakes, and stepping boldly into God's redemptive love.

DAY 8

TURNING FROM SIN

Scripture Reading:

"Repent therefore, and turn back, that your sins may be blotted out, that times of refreshing may come from the presence of the Lord." — **Acts 3:19 (ESV)**

"If my people, who are called by my name, will humble themselves and pray and seek my face and turn from their wicked ways, then I will hear from heaven, and I will forgive their sin and heal their land." — **2 Chronicles 7:14 (ESV)**

Repentance in the Heart of Lent

As we enter the second full week of Lent, the theme shifts toward **repentance and forgiveness**a fundamental aspect of the Lenten journey. True repentance is more than remorse or regret; it is a **decisive turning away from sin and turning toward God** with one's whole heart. In the Bible, the call to repent echoes repeatedly as an invitation to change direction—*to rethink our choices, reorient our hearts, and realign our lives with God's will*. In the original language of Scripture, the word often translated as *"repent"* **metanoia** literally means a **change of mind and life direction**.

In this season of Lent, we are invited to examine where we have clung to patterns, habits, or attitudes that separate us from God's purposes and peace. Today's devotional reminds us that **turning from sin is not merely about feeling sorry, but about embracing God's merciful call to transformation**. Repentance opens the door to refreshing from the Lord and deepens our communion with Him.

Reflection: Facing Sin, Choosing Renewal

Turning from sin begins with **recognition**. Just as the prophet Joel calls the people to *"return to the Lord"*, Lent calls us to honestly acknowledge those ways in which we have drifted from God's path. Repentance involves:

- **Acknowledging wrongdoing**
- **Feeling genuine sorrow over it**
- **Choosing to change direction**
- **Committing to walk in God's ways**

Repentance is not merely dwelling on guilt or shame. It is about **letting go of the old self** and stepping into the new life that God offers through Christ. A heartfelt repentance produces observable changes in both attitude and action — a life increasingly aligned with God's truth and love.

Consider:

- What recurring sin or pattern is God inviting you to leave behind?
- How is your heart responding — regret, resistance, or readiness to turn?
- What would it look like to step forward in obedience today?

Repentance transforms the heart and opens us to God's healing and renewing presence.

Meditation: A Change of Direction

Find a quiet place. Close your eyes and breathe deeply. Reflect on this declaration:

"Lord, show me where I need to turn back to You."

As you breathe in, imagine drawing God's light into your heart.
As you breathe out, imagine releasing what separates you from Him.

Repeat quietly:

*"Lord, have mercy.
Lord, change my heart."*

Allow the Holy Spirit to bring clarity and conviction—not condemnation—and let God's love lead you toward renewal.

Prayer

Loving and Merciful God,
Today I come before You with an open heart. I confess that there are ways I have wandered, habits I have embraced that do not reflect Your goodness, and thoughts that keep me far from Your peace.

Lord, show me where I need to turn from sin and turn toward You. Renew my mind, purify my intentions, and strengthen my resolve to walk in Your ways. Replace my old patterns with newness of life, that I may live in freedom and joy.

Thank You for Your forgiveness, Your patience, and Your steadfast love. Let today be a moment of repentance that leads to healing, restoration, and transformation.
In Jesus' name, Amen.

Words of Affirmation

Speak these declarations aloud or silently with faith:

- **I turn from what separates me from God and walk toward Him.**
- **God's mercy meets me and leads me to renewal.**
- **My repentance leads to peace and transformation.**
- **I am open to God's work in my heart today.**

Let these truths shape your perspective and steady your heart as you continue this Lent journey.

Application: Turning in Action

Today, take one intentional step of repentance:

- **Identify a specific sin or habit** you want to turn from.
- **Write it down**, then prayerfully commit it to God.
- **Choose a Scripture verse or prayer** that speaks to your repentance and repeat it throughout the day.
- **Seek reconciliation** if someone has been hurt by your actions.

Remember: repentance is a **lifelong journey**, not a single act of sorrow. Each step toward God brings deeper freedom and healing.

Closing Reflection

Turning from sin restores our relationship with God. Lent teaches us that repentance is not just about leaving the past behind — it is about stepping forward into the life God intends for us: a life marked by grace, love, and obedience.

As you continue this day of reflection, allow God's Spirit to guide you toward the renewal that only He can bring. May your heart be open, your steps directed by His truth, and your life transformed by His grace.

DAY 9

THE GIFT OF FORGIVENESS

Scripture Reading:

"Be kind to one another, tenderhearted, forgiving one another, as God in Christ has forgiven you." — **Ephesians 4:32 (ESV)**

"If we confess our sins, he is faithful and just to forgive us our sins and to cleanse us from all unrighteousness." — **1 John 1:9 (ESV)**

Understanding Forgiveness

Forgiveness is one of the most transformative gifts of the Christian life. On the ninth day of Lent, we pause to reflect on **God's forgiveness and our call to forgive others**. Forgiveness is not merely an action or a feeling; it is a **conscious choice to release resentment, anger, or the desire for revenge**, trusting God to handle justice and healing.

Lent reminds us that the journey of repentance and turning from sin is incomplete without forgiveness. God's mercy flows into our lives so that we can extend that same mercy to others. When we forgive, we reflect God's heart, release burdens that weigh down our souls, and create space for reconciliation and renewal.

Forgiveness is both **gift and discipline**. It transforms the forgiven and the forgiver, opening hearts to freedom, peace, and spiritual growth.

Reflection: Receiving and Giving Forgiveness

Forgiveness begins with acknowledging our own need for God's mercy. None of us are perfect, and all have fallen short (Romans 3:23). When we embrace the forgiveness God offers, we recognize His grace and become instruments of that grace toward others.

Consider these key aspects of forgiveness:

1. **Acknowledgment** — Recognize the hurt or offense without minimizing it.
2. **Release** — Let go of anger, bitterness, or desire for revenge.
3. **Prayer** — Ask God for the strength to forgive.
4. **Reconciliation** — Where possible, restore relationships with humility and love.

Reflect on your life:

- Is there someone you have been holding a grudge against?
- Are there past mistakes for which you struggle to forgive yourself?
- How might letting go of these burdens bring peace to your heart and life?

Forgiveness does not erase the past, but it **liberates the present and opens the door for God's work in the future**.

Meditation: Opening Your Heart

Find a quiet place and sit comfortably. Close your eyes and take several deep breaths. Imagine God's light filling the spaces in your heart that carry hurt, anger, or resentment.

Repeat silently:

"Lord, help me forgive as You have forgiven me."

Visualize releasing each person or situation you have struggled to forgive into God's care. Allow His love to wash over your heart, softening bitterness and replacing it with peace.

Prayer

Merciful God,
Thank You for the incredible gift of forgiveness in Christ. I confess my need for Your mercy and ask You to cleanse my heart from sin. Teach me to forgive as You have forgiven me, releasing resentment, anger, and bitterness.

Help me extend grace to others, even when it is difficult. Heal relationships that are broken, and restore hearts that are wounded. Let forgiveness transform my life, freeing me from the weight of grudges and filling me with Your peace.

May Your Spirit guide me to act with kindness, compassion, and mercy in all my relationships.
In Jesus' name, Amen.

Words of Affirmation

Speak these affirmations slowly, allowing them to sink into your heart:

- **I am forgiven and I forgive.**
- **God's mercy flows through me to others.**
- **I release resentment and embrace peace.**
- **Forgiveness opens my heart to God's love and freedom.**

Application: Practicing Forgiveness Today

1. **Identify one person** you need to forgive or reconcile with, even in prayer.

2. **Write a letter of forgiveness**, whether sent or private, expressing your willingness to release hurt.
3. **Forgive yourself** for mistakes or past failures; acknowledge that God's grace covers you.
4. **Act kindly** toward someone who has caused offense, letting your actions reflect God's mercy.

Forgiveness is both **an inward release and an outward act**. Each step you take in forgiving brings healing to your soul and aligns your heart with God's purposes.

Closing Reflection

The gift of forgiveness is life-changing. As we continue our Lenten journey, let us embrace both the forgiveness God extends to us and the forgiveness He calls us to offer. Forgiveness frees us from the chains of bitterness, restores relationships, and opens our hearts to deeper spiritual growth.

DAY 10

GRACE THAT CLEANSES

Scripture Reading:

"But if we walk in the light, as he is in the light, we have fellowship with one another, and the blood of Jesus his Son cleanses us from all sin." — **1 John 1:7 (NRSV)**

"Come now, let us reason together, says the Lord: though your sins are like scarlet, they shall be as white as snow; though they are red like crimson, they shall become like wool." — **Isaiah 1:18 (NRSV)**

Experiencing Cleansing Grace

On the tenth day of Lent, we reflect on **the cleansing power of God's grace**. Throughout the first two weeks of this devotional, we have explored surrender, repentance, and forgiveness. Today, we focus on the **transformative work of grace**—the divine power that purifies, restores, and renews our hearts.

Grace is not earned; it is freely given by God through Jesus Christ. It is the bridge between our sinfulness and God's holiness, the **washing that leaves us renewed and able to walk in light**. While repentance and confession prepare the heart, grace is what truly cleanses. It is both **gentle and powerful**, freeing us from guilt, shame, and the lingering effects of sin.

Lent invites us to **receive grace daily**, letting it penetrate every corner of our hearts. Just as physical cleansing removes dirt and grime, grace purifies the soul, leaving it fresh, vibrant, and ready to serve God fully.

Reflection: The Power of Grace

Consider the imagery in Isaiah 1:18: our sins may be deep and visible, yet God promises to transform even the darkest stain into purity. This promise is not conditional on our perfection but rests on His mercy.

Reflect today on these questions:

- In what areas of my life do I still carry guilt or shame?
- How can I actively receive God's cleansing grace today?
- What burdens am I holding that grace can release?

Grace cleanses by inviting honesty, humility, and trust. It does not merely forgive; it **renews our identity**, enabling us to live as God's children rather than as captives of past mistakes.

Meditation: Walking in the Light

Find a quiet place and close your eyes. Visualize yourself standing in a bright, pure light. Imagine God's cleansing grace flowing over you like a gentle stream, washing away every trace of sin, shame, and regret.

Silently repeat:

"Lord, cleanse me with Your grace. Make me new."

Breathe deeply, imagining each breath drawing in God's mercy and each exhale releasing guilt, fear, and heaviness.

Prayer

Merciful and Loving God,
Thank You for the cleansing power of Your grace. I confess the ways I have sinned and fallen short, and I ask You to wash my heart, mind, and spirit.

Renew me, Lord, that I may walk in Your light and live free from guilt and shame. Let Your grace transform every corner of my being, restoring joy, peace, and purpose. Teach me to extend Your grace to others as I have received it, and help me to live in the freedom and holiness You provide.

Thank You for the gift of cleansing, restoration, and hope. I surrender fully to Your renewing work today.
In Jesus' name, Amen.

Words of Affirmation

Say these aloud or silently, internalizing their truth:

- **God's grace cleanses me from all sin.**
- **I am renewed, restored, and made pure through Christ.**
- **Guilt and shame no longer define me.**
- **I receive God's mercy and walk in freedom.**

Application: Living in Cleansing Grace

1. **Identify an area of guilt or shame** and consciously give it to God in prayer.
2. **Journal a reflection** of God's forgiveness and cleansing, noting changes you desire in your life.

3. **Practice grace toward yourself and others**, forgiving fully and releasing judgment.
4. **Engage in a symbolic act of cleansing**, such as washing hands while meditating on God's grace removing sin and renewing your spirit.

Remember, grace is not a one-time event; it is **a continual source of renewal** throughout your Lenten journey and life.

Closing Reflection

God's grace cleanses and restores. It transforms hearts, removes shame, and empowers us to live in freedom. On this day, let us rest in the assurance that **no sin is too great for God's cleansing power**, and no past too dark for His light.

DAY 11

RENEWAL OF THE MIND

Scripture Reading:

"Do not be conformed to this world, but be transformed by the renewing of your mind, so that you may discern what is the will of God—what is good and acceptable and perfect." — **Romans 12:2 (NRSV)**

"Finally, brothers and sisters, whatever is true, whatever is honorable, whatever is just, whatever is pure, whatever is pleasing, whatever is commendable, if there is any excellence and if there is anything worthy of praise, think about these things." — **Philippians 4:8 (NRSV)**

Transforming Thought Patterns

As we move into Day 11 of our Lenten journey, we focus on the **renewal of the mind**. True transformation is not only about external behaviors or actions—it begins in the inner life, with our thoughts, perceptions, and attitudes. The Apostle Paul reminds us in Romans 12:2 that **renewing the mind is essential to discerning God's will** and living a life that reflects His goodness.

The mind is a battlefield where the patterns of sin, fear, and worldly influence often compete with the voice of God. Renewal involves intentionally **replacing destructive or negative thought patterns with godly, life-giving truths**. During Lent, this practice allows us to grow in discernment, wisdom, and spiritual clarity.

A renewed mind transforms how we interpret experiences, respond to challenges, and relate to others. It enables us to see situations through God's perspective rather than our own limited understanding.

Reflection: Aligning Thoughts with God's Truth

Consider the following reflective questions:

- What recurring thoughts or beliefs keep me anxious, fearful, or stuck in sin?
- How often do I allow worldly or harmful patterns to shape my perspective instead of God's Word?
- Which areas of my thinking need intentional surrender to God for renewal?

Renewing the mind is an active process. It involves:

1. **Scripture engagement** — immersing oneself in God's Word.
2. **Prayerful reflection** — asking the Holy Spirit to reveal unhelpful thought patterns.
3. **Meditation and contemplation** — replacing negativity with truth.
4. **Practice and discipline** — intentionally thinking and acting according to God's will.

Philippians 4:8 gives practical guidance: dwell on what is true, noble, right, pure, lovely, and praiseworthy. Each thought aligned with God brings clarity and spiritual strength.

Meditation: Transforming Thought Life

Find a quiet space and take several deep breaths. Close your eyes and reflect on Romans 12:2. Picture your mind as a garden: some areas are overgrown with weeds of fear, worry, and sin, while others are fertile for godly thoughts.

Silently pray:

"Lord, renew my mind. Remove thoughts that harm me and replace them with Your truth. Help me see the world as You see it."

Visualize God's light filling your mind, clearing away confusion, negativity, and false beliefs, leaving space for wisdom, peace, and discernment.

Prayer

Heavenly Father,
I ask You to renew my mind today. Remove any thoughts, doubts, or fears that lead me away from Your will. Transform my perspective so that I may discern what is good, acceptable, and perfect in Your eyes.

Teach me to dwell on truth, justice, purity, and praise. Help me filter every thought through Your Word and align my thinking with Your wisdom. Let my mind be a sanctuary of Your presence, guiding my actions, words, and decisions in accordance with Your love.

Thank You for the work of the Holy Spirit in my mind, renewing and transforming me daily.
In Jesus' name, Amen.

Words of Affirmation

- **My mind is being renewed by God's truth.**
- **I choose thoughts that honor God and promote peace.**
  - **The Holy Spirit guides my understanding and discernment.**
  - **I am transformed by the renewing of my mind each day.**

Application: Practicing Mind Renewal

1. **Scripture Focus** — Select one verse today to meditate on repeatedly, allowing it to shape your thoughts.
2. **Thought Audit** — Identify and challenge a recurring negative thought, replacing it with a biblical truth.
3. **Journaling** — Write down insights, prayers, and reflections from your meditation.
4. **Mindful Pause** — When faced with stress or temptation, pause and pray, asking God to renew your thinking.

Remember, renewing the mind is an ongoing practice that requires intentionality and reliance on God's Spirit.

Closing Reflection

A transformed mind leads to a transformed life. By surrendering unhealthy thought patterns and embracing God's truth, we gain clarity, freedom, and spiritual insight. Today, commit to letting God reshape your inner landscape so that your life may reflect His love, wisdom, and purpose.

DAY 12

REPAIRING BROKEN RELATIONSHIPS

Scripture Reading:

"If possible, so far as it depends on you, live peaceably with all." — **Romans 12:18 (NRSV)**

"Therefore, if you are offering your gift at the altar and there remember that your brother or sister has something against you, leave your gift there before the altar and go; first be reconciled to your brother or sister, and then come and offer your gift." — **Matthew 5:23–24 (NRSV)**

The Call to Reconciliation

On Day 12 of our Lenten journey, we focus on **repairing broken relationships**. Relationships are central to our humanity and our spiritual growth. Brokenness—whether caused by misunderstanding, offense, neglect, or sin—can weigh heavily on our hearts and hinder our fellowship with God and others.

Lent is a season of restoration, and God calls us to actively seek **reconciliation and peace**. Repairing relationships is not optional; it is a reflection of the forgiveness, grace, and mercy we have received through Christ. Just as God reconciles us to Himself, we are called to extend that reconciliation to others.

Repairing relationships does not always mean immediate resolution or even mutual agreement—it begins with **intention, humility, and a willingness to pursue peace**.

Reflection: Steps Toward Healing

Reflect on the state of your relationships. Consider these questions:

- Are there unresolved conflicts or tensions in my life?
- Have I withheld forgiveness or failed to seek it?
- What steps can I take to restore trust and peace?

Repairing broken relationships involves several key practices:

1. **Self-examination** — Acknowledge your role in the conflict and your need for God's guidance.
2. **Prayer** — Ask God to soften hearts, guide conversations, and bring understanding.
3. **Communication** — Approach the other person with humility, honesty, and grace.

4. **Forgiveness and Reconciliation** — Release resentment and pursue peace, even if full restoration takes time.

Romans 12:18 reminds us that **peace often depends on our willingness to act first**. This week of Lent invites us to take initiative in healing, reflecting God's love through reconciliation.

Meditation: Inviting God into Relationships

Find a quiet place and take several deep breaths. Close your eyes and picture the relationships that need healing. Visualize God standing beside you and the other person, holding both hearts in His care.

Silently pray:

"Lord, guide my words, soften my heart, and help me seek reconciliation. Heal what is broken and restore what is lost."

Breathe in God's grace; breathe out any bitterness or anger. Imagine His love bridging the gap and bringing understanding and peace.

Prayer

Gracious God,
I lift up the broken and strained relationships in my life. I confess my part in misunderstandings, offenses, or neglect. Help me to act with humility, patience, and love.

Teach me to forgive freely and seek forgiveness where I have hurt others. Guide my words, soften hearts, and grant wisdom to restore peace. May Your Spirit work in every relationship, bringing reconciliation, healing, and harmony.

Thank You for modeling forgiveness and restoration through Christ. Let my efforts reflect Your mercy and love in tangible ways.
In Jesus' name, Amen.

Words of Affirmation

- **I am committed to peace and reconciliation in my relationships.**
- **God's love guides my words and actions toward healing.**
- **I release bitterness and embrace forgiveness.**
- **Through Christ, broken relationships can be restored.**

Application: Practicing Reconciliation

1. **Identify one strained relationship** and pray for guidance in taking a step toward restoration.
2. **Reach out in humility**, whether through conversation, note, or act of kindness.

3. **Offer forgiveness or seek it** where needed, releasing past hurts to God.
4. **Commit to ongoing grace**, recognizing that restoration is often a process.

Remember, reconciliation begins with **intentional action**, guided by God's love and wisdom. Each step taken in humility and grace strengthens both your heart and the relationships around you.

Closing Reflection

Repairing broken relationships is a vital part of the Lenten journey. Just as God reconciles us to Himself, we are called to extend forgiveness and restoration to others. Today, take a step toward peace, allowing God to work through your heart, words, and actions.

DAY 13

EXTENDING FORGIVENESS TO OTHERS

Scripture Reading:

"And whenever you stand praying, forgive, if you have anything against anyone; so that your Father also who is in heaven may forgive you your trespasses." — **Mark 11:25 (NRSV)**

"Then Peter came and said to him, 'Lord, if another member of the church sins against me, how often should I forgive? As many as seven times?' Jesus said to him, 'Not seven times, but seventy-seven times.'" — **Matthew 18:21–22 (NRSV)**

The Call to Forgive

On Day 13 of our Lenten journey, the focus shifts from receiving forgiveness to **extending forgiveness to others**. Forgiveness is a cornerstone of the Christian life—not optional but essential for spiritual health. Just as God has forgiven us fully and freely, we are called to release the offenses of others and walk in reconciliation.

Extending forgiveness is not always easy. It can feel counterintuitive, especially when we have been deeply hurt or wronged. Yet Scripture emphasizes that **our willingness to forgive reflects our understanding of God's mercy**. To forgive is to participate in God's work of restoration, freeing both the offended and the offender from the bondage of resentment.

Lent reminds us that forgiveness is a daily choice—a step of obedience, humility, and love. By forgiving others, we echo the grace we have received and make room for God to continue His transformative work in our hearts.

Reflection: The Heart of Forgiveness

Forgiveness is a process, not a single act. Consider the following:

- **Recognition of hurt** — Acknowledge the offense honestly without minimizing or ignoring it.
- **Release of resentment** — Let go of the desire for revenge or retribution.
- **Prayer for the other person** — Ask God to bless, guide, and transform them.
- **Restoration of peace** — Seek reconciliation if possible, but trust God even if reconciliation is not immediate.

Reflective questions:

- Who in my life needs my forgiveness?
- Am I holding on to grudges that hinder my spiritual growth?
- How can I extend grace, even when it is difficult?

Forgiveness liberates the heart, allowing God's love and peace to flow more freely in all areas of life. Matthew 18:22 reminds us that forgiveness is not limited; it is **continuous, generous, and unconditional**, mirroring God's mercy toward us.

Meditation: Preparing to Forgive

Sit quietly and close your eyes. Visualize the person or situation you need to forgive. Place them in God's hands and silently repeat:

"Lord, help me forgive as You have forgiven me. Remove bitterness and fill my heart with Your love."

Take a deep breath in, imagining God's grace flowing into your heart. Exhale, releasing anger, resentment, and the need to hold the offense. Repeat this process as many times as needed until your heart feels lighter and your spirit more at peace.

Prayer

Gracious and Merciful God,
I confess that there are people I have struggled to forgive. I carry hurt, resentment, and bitterness that weigh heavily on my heart. Today, I choose to release them to You.

Lord, help me forgive as You have forgiven me. Teach me to extend mercy freely, without judgment or conditions. Heal the wounds in my relationships and transform my heart with Your love. May my willingness to forgive reflect Your grace and draw others closer to You.

Thank You for the freedom, peace, and restoration that forgiveness brings. Let my life be a testament to Your mercy.
In Jesus' name, Amen.

Words of Affirmation

- **I release all bitterness and choose forgiveness.**
- **God's grace empowers me to forgive fully and freely.**
- **Forgiveness restores my heart and opens the way for peace.**
- **I reflect God's mercy in my relationships through forgiveness.**

Application: Practicing Forgiveness Today

1. **Identify one person** you need to forgive and commit to releasing resentment through prayer.
2. **Write a letter or journal entry** expressing forgiveness, whether or not you send it.
3. **Take a concrete step toward reconciliation**, even if it is a small act of kindness or reaching out in prayer for them.
4. **Reflect on God's forgiveness in your life**, remembering how freely and fully He has forgiven you.

Forgiveness is not about condoning wrong behavior but about **choosing freedom and peace** in obedience to God's Word.

Closing Reflection

Extending forgiveness is a profound spiritual discipline that mirrors the mercy God has shown us. Today, take deliberate steps to release offense, trust God with justice, and reflect His grace in your relationships.

DAY 14

THE FREEDOM OF FORGIVENESS

Scripture Reading:

"So if the Son makes you free, you will be free indeed." — **John 8:36 (NRSV)**

"Blessed is the one whose transgression is forgiven, whose sin is covered." — **Psalm 32:1 (NRSV)**

Experiencing the Freedom of Forgiveness

On Day 14 of our Lenten journey, we pause to reflect on the **freedom that forgiveness brings**. By this point, we have explored repentance, God's cleansing grace, and the act of forgiving others. Today invites us to **internalize and celebrate the liberation that forgiveness provides**—both the forgiveness we have received from God and the forgiveness we have extended to others.

Forgiveness is not just an ethical duty or a spiritual practice—it is a **pathway to freedom**. Holding onto resentment, guilt, or anger binds the heart, distorts our thinking, and hinders our relationship with God and others. By embracing forgiveness fully, we experience **release, renewal, and restoration**, enabling us to live in the lightness of God's grace.

Lent calls us to freedom—not in the absence of struggle, but in the presence of God's redeeming work. Freedom begins in the heart and mind, as we surrender all offense, hurt, and guilt to Christ.

Reflection: The Transformative Power of Forgiveness

Forgiveness is a gift we receive and a gift we give. Reflect on the following:

- **Receiving Forgiveness:** God's forgiveness cleanses, covers, and restores. Accepting it removes the burden of guilt and shame, giving peace that surpasses understanding.
- **Extending Forgiveness:** Letting go of resentment or anger toward others allows God's love to flow through us, restoring relationships and opening the heart to deeper joy.
- **Freedom in Action:** Forgiveness is liberating—it releases the past and allows us to live fully in the present.

Consider these questions:

- Have I fully embraced God's forgiveness for myself?

- Am I holding on to any lingering anger toward others?
- How can I live today in the freedom that forgiveness provides?

Psalm 32 reminds us that forgiveness brings **blessing, relief, and restored joy**, while John 8:36 affirms that true freedom is found in Christ.

Meditation: Embracing Freedom

Find a quiet space and close your eyes. Visualize the burdens you have been carrying—offenses, guilt, shame, or resentment. See Christ standing before you, offering His hand.

Silently repeat:

"Lord, I receive Your forgiveness. I release all offense. I embrace Your freedom."

Breathe deeply. Imagine the chains of resentment and guilt falling away, leaving your spirit light, peaceful, and renewed. Stay in silence for a few moments, basking in God's liberating presence.

Prayer

Merciful and Loving God,
Thank You for the gift of forgiveness that frees my heart, mind, and spirit. I confess the burdens I have carried, the resentment I have held, and the guilt I have felt.

Today, I choose to accept Your forgiveness fully and release all offense and bitterness toward others. Cleanse my heart, renew my mind, and restore my soul to peace.

Help me walk in the freedom You provide, living each day in Your love, mercy, and grace. May my life reflect the liberation that comes through Christ, inspiring reconciliation, joy, and hope. In Jesus' name, Amen.

Words of Affirmation

- **I am forgiven, and I live in the freedom of God's grace.**
- **I release all resentment and embrace peace.**
- **God's mercy transforms my heart and restores my joy.**
- **I walk in freedom, empowered by Christ's love.**

Application: Living in Forgiveness

1. **Reflect** on the freedom God has given you through forgiveness.
2. **Let go of one lingering grudge or resentment**, consciously releasing it to God.
3. **Celebrate restored relationships** or the peace that comes from letting go.
4. **Share the gift of forgiveness** with someone today, through prayer, words, or actions.

Forgiveness is not passive; it is an **active embrace of freedom and grace**, allowing God to transform both your heart and your relationships.

Closing Reflection

The freedom of forgiveness is one of the most profound gifts of the Lenten journey. By releasing guilt, resentment, and offense, we step into a life of peace, lightness, and restored connection with God and others.

WEEK 3

PRAYER AND CONTEMPLATION

Theme: Deepening Communion with God
Scripture Focus: *"Seek first the kingdom of God and his righteousness, and all these things will be added to you."* — Matthew 6:33

Week 3 of our Lenten journey invites us into **prayer and contemplation**, focusing on developing a deeper, more intimate communion with God. While the first two weeks centered on surrender, repentance, and forgiveness, this week emphasizes **listening to God, seeking His guidance, and resting in His presence**.

Prayer is more than a ritual—it is a **dialogue with the Divine**, an intentional practice of aligning our hearts and minds with God's will. Contemplation deepens this experience, creating space to hear God's voice, reflect on His Word, and be transformed by His Spirit.

Throughout this week, Scripture reminds us that seeking God earnestly opens the heart to wisdom, peace, and spiritual clarity. As we devote time to prayer, meditation, and reflection, we cultivate a **habit of noticing God's presence in everyday life**, allowing Him to guide our thoughts, decisions, and actions.

This week encourages:

- **Intentional prayer** — talking to God with honesty, reverence, and openness.
- **Listening in silence** — practicing stillness to hear God's voice.
- **Reflection on Scripture** — allowing God's Word to illuminate daily life.
- **Journaling or contemplation** — recording insights, prayers, and divine guidance.

DAY 15

SILENCE AND SOLITUDE

Scripture Reading:

"Be still, and know that I am God." — **Psalm 46:10 (ESV)**

"Very early in the morning, while it was still dark, Jesus got up, left the house, and went out to a solitary place, where he prayed." — **Mark 1:35 (ESV)**

Communion in the Quiet

As we begin **Week 3 - Prayer and Contemplation**, today we focus on one of the most essential, yet often overlooked, spiritual disciplines: **silence and solitude**. In the rhythm of everyday life, we are constantly surrounded by noise, tasks, and internal chatter. Yet Scripture invites us into *intentional stillness and quietness*—not as an escape, but as a sacred space where we can listen deeply to God's voice and feel His presence.

Jesus Himself modeled this practice throughout His earthly ministry. In moments of pressure, decision, and preparation, He often withdrew to quiet, solitary places to pray (Mark 1:35, Luke 5:16). These silent retreats were not passive breaks but **active engagements of the soul with the Divine**. Silence provided Jesus the space to commune with His Father, orient His heart toward God's will, and receive strength for the days ahead.

Silence and solitude are not just spiritual luxuries; they are *essentials for transformation*. This discipline reminds us that noise distracts while stillness reveals—God's truths, God's presence, and God's guiding whispers are most clearly heard when we quiet both the world and our inner selves.

Reflection: Entering the Sacred Quiet

Silence is more than the absence of sound; it is a **welcoming of God's presence** into the depths of our hearts. Solitude is not loneliness; it is being alone *with God*, fully present and attentive to Him. In silence, we stop telling God what we want and begin to **listen for what God wants to tell us**.

God often speaks in the quiet:

- When our frantic striving fades
- When we are not chasing answers
- When we simply *wait* on Him

Isaiah reminds us that **quietness and trust are where salvation and strength are found** (see *Isaiah 30:15*). In stillness, we learn to trust God rather than our own solutions.

Reflection questions to ponder today:

- What distractions occupy your inner world most often?
- Where are you tempted to fill silence with activity instead of prayer?
- What might God be calling you to hear if you simply *stop and listen*?

Meditation: Practicing Stillness

Find a quiet place—perhaps early morning or a peaceful moment in your day. Sit comfortably and **breathe slowly**. With each breath, invite God's presence into your heart.

Silently repeat:

"Be still before You, Lord."

Let go of distractions. Let God's presence fill the silence.

Imagine drawing close to Jesus as He prayed alone in the early morning light. Let silence become a bridge between your heart and God's presence.

Prayer

Holy and Eternal God,
You speak in the stillness of our hearts and the quiet of our souls. Today, I step into silence and solitude before You. Remove the noise that distracts me and help me to rest in Your presence.

Teach me to listen deeply, not merely to the sound of my own voice, but to the quiet whisper of Your Spirit. As Jesus withdrew to pray, let me, too, find strength, clarity, and communion with You in stillness.

Help me trust that You are near even when all else is silent. May my heart be attuned to Your voice, and may Your peace settle over me as I linger in Your presence.
In Jesus' name, Amen.

Words of Affirmation

Speak these truths slowly and let them settle into your soul:

- **In silence, I hear God's voice more clearly.**
- **Solitude draws me closer to the heart of God.**
- **I am loved, seen, and held by God even in quiet moments.**
- **Stillness brings peace to my spirit and clarity to my mind.**

Application: Practicing Silence and Solitude Today

1. Start Small—Begin with 5–10 minutes:
Choose a quiet place. Turn off your phone or notifications. Sit in stillness and simply *be* before God.

2. Quiet Prayer Walk:
Walk outdoors without music or distraction. Let nature's silence deepen your awareness of God's presence.

3. Journaling in Solitude:
After a period of silence, write what you sensed God revealing—words, feelings, thoughts, or gentle nudges of the Spirit.

4. Reflect on Jesus' Practice:
Consider how Jesus made space for quiet throughout His ministry (Mark 1:35). What might He want to say to you in your solitude today?

Silence is not emptiness—it is *space filled with God's presence*. The more we practice stillness, the more readily we recognize God's voice amidst life's noise.

Closing Reflection: A Sacred Invitation

God's invitation to silence and solitude is not about withdrawal from life; it is about **entrance into deeper communion with Him**. In silence, the soul learns to abide, to trust, to listen, and to be shaped by the presence of the Almighty.

Today, let your heart rest in God. Let the quiet be your companion and let His voice become the most familiar sound you know.

DAY 16

PRAYING WITHOUT CEASING

Scripture Reading:

"Rejoice always, pray without ceasing, give thanks in all circumstances; for this is the will of God in Christ Jesus for you." — **1 Thessalonians 5:16-18 (ESV)**

"Devote yourselves to prayer, being watchful and thankful." — **Colossians 4:2 (NRSV)**

Living a Life of Prayer

On Day 16 of our Lenten journey, we focus on **praying without ceasing**—a call to cultivate a continuous, intimate conversation with God throughout our daily lives. Prayer is not limited to formal moments of devotion or quiet times in the morning or evening. Rather, it is **an ongoing dialogue, an orientation of the heart toward God, and a lifestyle of communion**.

The Apostle Paul encourages believers to rejoice, pray constantly, and give thanks in all circumstances. This does not mean speaking endlessly or mechanically but **keeping a spirit of prayer alive** in every thought, decision, and interaction. Such a practice deepens our reliance on God, strengthens spiritual awareness, and transforms ordinary moments into sacred opportunities.

Praying without ceasing is a discipline that fosters **mindfulness, gratitude, and dependence on God**, helping us navigate challenges, discern His will, and experience His sustaining presence in every aspect of life.

Reflection: Integrating Prayer into Daily Life

Consider these reflections for cultivating a continuous prayerful heart:

- **Constant Conversation:** Approach daily tasks—work, chores, interactions—with a prayerful mindset. Speak to God naturally, asking for guidance, wisdom, and strength.
- **Gratitude as Prayer:** Transform routine gratitude into prayer. Every small blessing becomes an opportunity to praise and acknowledge God's goodness.
- **Prayer in Action:** Prayer can accompany action. Before making a decision, express dependence on God; while encountering difficulties, ask for patience and wisdom.
- **Listening as Prayer:** Prayer is not just speaking—it is also attentively listening for God's guidance, inspiration, and comfort.

Reflection questions:

- How often do I pause to include God in ordinary moments of my day?
- What distractions prevent me from cultivating a continual prayerful mindset?
- In what ways can I make prayer a natural, constant part of my life?

Continuous prayer does not demand perfection but encourages **intentionality and responsiveness to God's presence** in every moment.

Meditation: Practicing Unceasing Prayer

Find a comfortable space and take a few slow, deep breaths. Focus on the idea that God is always near. Picture a **cord of prayer connecting your heart to God's presence throughout your day**.

Silently repeat:

"Lord, I lift my heart to You in every moment. Be with me, guide me, and strengthen me."

As thoughts arise, let them become prayers—short, sincere, and connected to God's presence. Practice lifting your mind to Him during daily routines, trusting that even brief moments of awareness count as prayer.

Prayer

Heavenly Father,
Thank You for inviting me into constant communion with You. Teach me to pray without ceasing—not merely with words, but with a heart attuned to Your presence in every situation.

Help me see daily tasks, relationships, and challenges as opportunities to connect with You. Remind me to lift prayers of gratitude, seek guidance in decisions, and trust You in moments of uncertainty.

May my heart remain watchful, my spirit thankful, and my life a continuous offering of devotion to You. Let prayer transform not only my moments of stillness but also my actions, words, and thoughts.
In Jesus' name, Amen.

Words of Affirmation

- **I am in constant communion with God through prayer.**
- **Every moment is an opportunity to speak and listen to God.**
- **Gratitude and awareness cultivate continuous prayer.**
- **God's presence surrounds me, guiding and sustaining me always.**

Application: Practicing Praying Without Ceasing

1. **Start small:** Begin with brief prayers during routine tasks cooking, commuting, or walking.
2. **Use reminders:** Place visual cues (like sticky notes or phone reminders) to pause and lift a prayer.
3. **Incorporate gratitude:** Each time you notice a blessing, thank God aloud or silently.
4. **Reflect at day's end:** Review moments where God's guidance or presence was felt, acknowledging His faithfulness.

Praying without ceasing is not about perfection but about cultivating **a heart that naturally turns to God throughout life's rhythms**, allowing prayer to become both spontaneous and continuous.

Closing Reflection

Living in unceasing prayer deepens intimacy with God and transforms ordinary life into sacred moments. By weaving prayer into every thought, action, and decision, we experience constant guidance, peace, and joy.

DAY 17

LISTENING FOR GOD'S VOICE

Scripture Reading:

"My sheep hear my voice. I know them, and they follow me." — **John 10:27 (NRSV)**

"Be still before the Lord and wait patiently for him; do not fret when people succeed in their ways, when they carry out their wicked schemes." — **Psalm 37:7 (NRSV)**

Introduction: Tuning Our Hearts to God

On Day 17 of our Lenten journey, we focus on **listening for God's voice**—a crucial component of prayer and contemplation. While prayer often involves speaking to God, listening is equally vital. God desires **an ongoing relationship** with us, and His guidance, wisdom, and comfort are communicated when we intentionally **pause, quiet our hearts, and attune our ears to Him**.

In John 10:27, Jesus assures us that His followers can recognize His voice. But hearing requires **practice, patience, and attentiveness**. In the busyness of life, the spiritual "noise" of distraction, anxiety, or self-interest can drown out God's subtle whispers. Lent invites us to **develop the discipline of listening**, creating a sacred space where God's voice becomes clear, trusted, and life-giving.

Listening to God is not passive. It involves **active presence, reflective prayer, and openness to His guidance**, whether through Scripture, the prompting of the Holy Spirit, or circumstances in our daily lives.

Reflection: Recognizing God's Voice

Consider these ways God often communicates:

- **Through Scripture:** His Word is alive, offering guidance, correction, and encouragement.
- **Through the Holy Spirit:** God speaks inwardly, nudging our conscience, inspiring thoughts, or prompting action.
- **Through Circumstances:** Sometimes God's direction comes through opportunities, doors, or gentle closures in life.
- **Through Others:** God can speak through wise counsel, encouragement, or even loving correction from others.

Reflection questions:

- How often do I pause long enough to hear God's guidance?
- In what areas of life am I leaning on my own understanding instead of seeking God's direction?
- How can I cultivate the patience and stillness needed to discern His voice?

Listening requires **intentional slowing down**, a humble acknowledgment that God's wisdom surpasses our own, and trust that His guidance is always for our good.

Meditation: Practicing Spiritual Listening

Find a quiet, comfortable place. Close your eyes and take several deep breaths. Visualize God standing before you, speaking gently and personally.

Silently repeat:

"Lord, I open my heart to hear Your voice. Teach me to listen and follow."

Breathe deeply and allow your mind to release distractions. Listen attentively for a thought, feeling, or Scripture that arises. Be patient—hearing God may take time and repeated practice. Trust that even small impressions are meaningful.

Prayer

Loving and Wise God,
I desire to hear Your voice today. Help me quiet my heart and mind so that I may recognize Your guidance in every area of my life. Teach me to discern Your whispers above the noise of the world.

Give me patience to wait, humility to trust, and courage to obey when I hear Your direction. Open my ears, heart, and spirit to Your wisdom. May my life reflect Your voice in the words I speak, the choices I make, and the love I extend to others.

Thank You for speaking to me and for Your constant presence. I trust that You are guiding me even when I cannot yet fully perceive Your direction.
In Jesus' name, Amen.

Words of Affirmation

- **I am attuned to the voice of God in my life.**
- **I hear and recognize His guidance in Scripture, Spirit, and circumstances.**
- **God speaks to me daily, and I respond with trust and obedience.**
- **I am patient and attentive to His gentle whispers.**

Application: Hearing God in Daily Life

1. **Set aside intentional quiet time** to listen to God, even for 5–10 minutes.
2. **Journal impressions** or insights received during prayer or meditation.
3. **Practice discernment** by comparing impressions with Scripture and seeking counsel if needed.
4. **Act on guidance received**, trusting that obedience deepens intimacy with God.
5. **Observe God's voice in everyday circumstances**, recognizing that He speaks in both subtle and obvious ways.

Remember, listening is a skill developed over time. Each small moment of attentiveness strengthens your spiritual sensitivity and deepens your communion with God.

Closing Reflection

Hearing God's voice transforms prayer from monologue to dialogue and deepens our Lenten journey. As we cultivate the discipline of listening, we grow in **trust, wisdom, and obedience**, allowing God's presence to guide every step.

DAY 18

PETITION-ASKING, SEEKING, KNOCKING

Scripture Reading:

"Ask, and it will be given to you; seek, and you will find; knock, and it will be opened to you. For everyone who asks receives, and the one who seeks finds, and to the one who knocks it will be opened." — **Matthew 7:7-8 (NRSV)**

"You do not have, because you do not ask." — **James 4:2 (NRSV)**

The Power of Petition in Prayer

On Day 18 of our Lenten journey, we focus on **petition**—bringing our requests, needs, and desires before God. Petition is a vital aspect of prayer that demonstrates **dependence on God** and acknowledges Him as the ultimate source of provision, wisdom, and strength.

Jesus teaches us to *ask, seek, and knock* with confidence, persistence, and faith. Petition is not about demanding God's will to match ours but **aligning our desires with His perfect purposes**. Through petition, we cultivate humility, trust, and expectancy, recognizing that God knows our needs even before we voice them (Matthew 6:8).

Lent is a season of reflection and spiritual renewal, making it an ideal time to practice **intentional petition**—lifting both our personal needs and the needs of others to the throne of grace.

Reflection: Bringing Needs Before God

Petition teaches us several spiritual truths:

- **Dependence:** Prayer reminds us that we are not self-sufficient. God is our source.
- **Persistence:** Repeatedly seeking God demonstrates faith and trust in His timing.
- **Alignment:** As we ask, God shapes our hearts, helping us discern which requests align with His will.

Reflection questions:

- What needs, desires, or burdens have I hesitated to bring before God?

- How can I approach petition prayer with humility rather than entitlement?
- Do I trust God's timing and wisdom when my requests are not immediately answered?

Petition is a sacred exercise of faith, teaching us to rely on God while surrendering outcomes to His wisdom.

Meditation: Practicing Asking, Seeking, and Knocking

Find a quiet space and take a few deep breaths. Picture yourself standing before God's throne with open hands and a heart ready to receive His guidance.

Silently pray:

"Lord, I bring my needs, concerns, and desires before You. Teach me to ask with faith, seek with persistence, and knock with hope, trusting Your perfect will."

Visualize yourself asking confidently, seeking diligently, and knocking persistently. Sense God's openness and willingness to hear, knowing that His answers may be immediate, delayed, or differently shaped than expected, always in alignment with His perfect plan.

Prayer

Gracious Father,
I come before You with my petitions, trusting that You hear every word and know every need. Teach me to ask with faith, seek with persistence, and knock with hope. Help me to surrender my desires to Your will, trusting that You provide according to Your wisdom and love.

I bring my personal needs and the needs of others before You today. Strengthen my faith to persevere in prayer, even when answers are delayed or unexpected. May my heart remain aligned with Your will, and may I grow in trust, patience, and reliance on Your grace.

Thank You for hearing me, guiding me, and answering in ways that bring eternal good.
In Jesus' name, Amen.

Words of Affirmation

- **I bring my needs and desires before God with faith and trust.**
- **God hears every prayer and answers according to His perfect wisdom.**
- **I persist in prayer, knowing that He is faithful.**
- **Asking, seeking, and knocking deepens my relationship with God.**

Application: Practicing Petition Today

1. **List your petitions**—personal, relational, or spiritual needs. Pray over each one intentionally.

2. **Seek God's guidance**—ask Him to reveal His will regarding your requests.
3. **Knock with persistence**—commit to praying daily, not losing heart if the answer is delayed.
4. **Include others in your petitions**—lift up friends, family, community, and even global needs.

Remember, petition is an invitation to **engage with God actively and trust Him deeply**, transforming both your heart and your perspective as you wait on His answers.

Closing Reflection

Petition invites us to approach God with **bold faith and humble hearts**. Asking, seeking, and knocking is not merely about getting answers; it is about **growing in intimacy, trust, and alignment with God's will**.

DAY 19

GRATITUDE THROUGH THE STORM

Scripture Reading:

"Give thanks in all circumstances; for this is the will of God in Christ Jesus for you." — **1 Thessalonians 5:18 (NRSV)**

"Though the mountains be shaken and the hills be removed, yet my unfailing love for you will not be shaken." — **Isaiah 54:10 (NRSV)**

Embracing Gratitude in Difficult Times

On Day 19 of our Lenten journey, we focus on **gratitude through the storm**. Life often brings trials, challenges, and uncertainties—times when it seems nearly impossible to rejoice. Yet Scripture reminds us that **thankfulness is not dependent on circumstances but on God's unchanging goodness**.

Gratitude in hardship is a spiritual discipline that strengthens faith, cultivates resilience, and anchors the soul in God's promises. Paul instructs believers to give thanks in *all* circumstances, highlighting that gratitude is an active choice, a conscious surrender of perspective to God even when the situation is challenging.

Lent is a season of reflection and renewal. By practicing gratitude through trials, we **acknowledge God's sovereignty, recognize His sustaining presence, and experience a deeper peace that transcends difficulties**.

Reflection: Finding Blessings Amid Trials

When storms arise, gratitude transforms perspective:

- **Shifts Focus:** Gratitude redirects attention from problems to God's provision.
- **Strengthens Faith:** Thankfulness in trials reinforces trust in God's plan.
- **Cultivates Joy:** Even small blessings become sources of hope and encouragement.
- **Fosters Spiritual Growth:** Storms are opportunities to develop endurance, patience, and reliance on God.

Reflection questions:

- What challenges am I facing that make gratitude difficult?
- How can I intentionally identify God's blessings today, even amid struggle?

- In what ways has God been faithful during previous storms in my life?

Isaiah 54:10 reminds us that **God's love and faithfulness remain steadfast**, even when circumstances are shaken. Gratitude is not an escape from reality but a declaration of trust in His enduring goodness.

Meditation: Practicing Gratitude

Sit in a quiet space and close your eyes. Take a deep breath and visualize a storm around you—representing challenges, worries, or fears. Now imagine God standing with you, His light piercing the darkness.

Silently repeat:

"Lord, I choose to see Your blessings even in this storm. Thank You for Your unfailing love and faithfulness."

Breathe in His peace and exhale anxiety. List mentally three things you are grateful for today—perhaps relationships, provision, strength, or hope. Let each act of gratitude **lighten your heart and bring calm** to your spirit.

Prayer

Faithful God,
In the midst of trials and storms, I choose to lift my heart in gratitude. Thank You for Your unchanging love, Your provision, and Your presence that never leaves me.

Help me recognize Your blessings, even when circumstances are difficult. Strengthen my faith and cultivate a spirit of thankfulness that persists through challenges. May gratitude become a lens through which I view every situation, drawing me closer to You and filling my heart with peace.

Thank You, Lord, for being my refuge, my strength, and my hope. Let my life reflect gratitude, even when the world around me is turbulent.
In Jesus' name, Amen.

Words of Affirmation

- **I give thanks in all circumstances, trusting God's plan.**
- **God's love is steadfast, even in my storms.**
- **Gratitude transforms my perspective and strengthens my faith.**
- **I choose joy and peace through God's unchanging grace.**

Application: Practicing Gratitude Through Challenges

1. **Identify one trial or difficulty** and consciously give thanks for God's presence in it.
2. **Journal three blessings** you notice today, even small ones.
3. **Share gratitude with others**—encouragement spreads hope and perspective.
4. **Reflect daily on God's faithfulness** in past challenges, building trust for present storms.

Gratitude in hardship is **an act of faith**, acknowledging God's sovereignty and finding peace in His presence, even when the world feels uncertain.

Closing Reflection

Gratitude is a powerful spiritual discipline, especially during trials. By intentionally giving thanks through storms, we **strengthen our trust, anchor our hearts in God's love, and cultivate joy that transcends circumstances**.

DAY 20

ADORATION-WORSHIP IN TRUTH

Scripture Reading:

"God is spirit, and those who worship him must worship in spirit and truth." — **John 4:24 (NRSV)**

"Let everything that has breath praise the Lord! Praise the Lord!" — **Psalm 150:6 (ESV)**

Worship as a Lifestyle

On Day 20 of our Lenten journey, we focus on **adoration—worship in truth**. Adoration is the heart's response to God's greatness, love, and faithfulness. It goes beyond singing songs or attending services; it is **a posture of reverence, awe, and surrender that permeates every aspect of our lives**.

Jesus reminds us that true worship is **both in spirit and in truth**. Spiritually, it requires a heart attuned to God's presence. Practically, it is expressed through integrity, obedience, and sincerity. Lent is a season of reflection and renewal, and adoration invites us to **reconnect with God's majesty, acknowledge His worth, and cultivate heartfelt worship** in both private devotion and public life.

Worship in truth is transformative—it shapes our thoughts, decisions, and actions, aligning our entire being with God's purposes. Through adoration, we remember that God is worthy of all praise, not because of what He does for us alone, but because of who He is—holy, faithful, and eternal.

Reflection: Experiencing God Through Adoration

Consider the following truths about worship and adoration:

- **God's Nature Inspires Worship:** His love, wisdom, and power invite us to honor Him daily.
- **Worship as Alignment:** Adoration aligns our hearts with God's truth, fostering humility and surrender.
- **Adoration Through Life:** Worship is not only expressed in song; it is reflected in obedience, service, and gratitude.
- **Spiritual Renewal:** Daily adoration refreshes our spirits, strengthens faith, and encourages steadfastness in trials.

Reflection questions:

- How do I express adoration to God in my daily life?
- Are there areas where my worship is routine rather than heartfelt?
- How can I cultivate worship that is both in spirit and in truth?

Psalm 150 reminds us to let **everything that has breath praise the Lord**, emphasizing that worship is a holistic response encompassing all of life.

Meditation: Cultivating a Heart of Adoration

Sit quietly and focus on God's greatness. Visualize His majesty, love, and faithfulness surrounding you. Let your heart respond naturally with awe and reverence.

Silently repeat:

"Lord, I worship You in spirit and in truth. Your greatness and love inspire my heart to adore You."

Consider the ways God has revealed Himself in your life—through creation, provision, answered prayers, or daily blessings. Allow gratitude and awe to rise as a natural expression of worship.

Prayer

Holy and Majestic God,
I lift my heart in adoration and praise. You are holy, faithful, and eternal. I worship You in spirit and in truth, acknowledging Your greatness and love.

Teach me to live a life of worship beyond words—through my actions, my choices, and my devotion. Let adoration flow from my heart in every circumstance, transforming my thoughts, decisions, and relationships.

Thank You for Your presence, Your guidance, and Your unchanging faithfulness. May my life be a reflection of true worship, honoring You in spirit, truth, and every breath I take.
In Jesus' name, Amen.

Words of Affirmation

- **I worship God in spirit and in truth.**
- **Adoration flows naturally from a heart aligned with God.**
- **I honor God through my words, actions, and thoughts.**
- **Worship renews my spirit and strengthens my faith.**

Application: Practicing Adoration Today

1. **Spend intentional time in worship**—through song, Scripture, or silent meditation on God's attributes.
2. **Express adoration through actions**—serve, bless, or encourage someone today as an act of worship.
3. **Record ways God has revealed Himself** in your life, reflecting on His goodness, faithfulness, and majesty.
4. **Incorporate worship into daily routines**—turn mundane tasks into offerings of praise to God.

Adoration is not limited to special moments; it is a **continuous lifestyle of praise and reverence**, shaping every aspect of our journey with God.

Closing Reflection

Worship in spirit and truth transforms our hearts, minds, and actions. Through adoration, we encounter God's presence, align with His will, and experience renewal in every area of life.

DAY 21

THE PRACTICE OF WAITING

Scripture Reading:

"Wait for the Lord; be strong, and let your heart take courage; wait for the Lord!" — **Psalm 27:14 (NRSV)**

"But if we hope for what we do not see, we wait for it with patience." — **Romans 8:25 (NRSV)**

Embracing the Discipline of Waiting

On Day 21 of our Lenten journey, we pause to reflect on **the practice of waiting**. Waiting is often uncomfortable, challenging, and countercultural in a world that prizes speed, immediacy, and control. Yet Scripture consistently invites us to **wait on the Lord**, trusting His timing, wisdom, and faithfulness.

Waiting is not passive idleness; it is an **active spiritual discipline**. It cultivates patience, strengthens faith, and refines character. In waiting, we learn to surrender our timelines, desires, and control to God, recognizing that His purposes are higher than our own. Lent, as a season of reflection, provides the perfect framework to practice this sacred discipline.

When we wait on God, we align our hearts with His will, develop **trust in His providence**, and open ourselves to His transformative work. Waiting becomes a space for spiritual growth, prayerful reflection, and deepened intimacy with God.

Reflection: Lessons in Waiting

Waiting teaches profound spiritual truths:

- **Trust in God's Timing:** God's plans unfold perfectly, even if they do not align with ours.
- **Patience Cultivates Strength:** Waiting develops resilience, endurance, and reliance on God.
- **Opportunities for Prayer:** In times of waiting, our hearts turn naturally to God in dependence and dialogue.
- **Refinement of Character:** Waiting shapes humility, gratitude, and surrender, molding us into Christlike individuals.

Reflection questions:

- Where in my life am I struggling to wait for God's guidance or provision?
- How can I turn periods of waiting into opportunities for prayer, reflection, and trust?

- What lessons has God taught me in past seasons of waiting?

Romans 8:25 reminds us that **hope and patience go hand in hand**. Waiting is not wasted time—it is an active engagement with God's promises, trusting that what He has prepared is worth the pause.

Meditation: Practicing Spiritual Waiting

Find a quiet space and sit comfortably. Close your eyes and take several deep breaths. Imagine yourself **surrendering your timeline, desires, and control to God**, placing your life fully in His hands.

Silently repeat:

"Lord, I wait for You with patience, trusting Your timing and Your plans."

Focus on releasing anxiety, impatience, or frustration. Visualize God's faithful presence surrounding you, giving peace and reassurance. Let the waiting become a **sacred space of reflection, prayer, and surrender**.

Prayer

Faithful God,
I confess that waiting is often difficult and uncomfortable. I struggle to trust Your timing and surrender my desires fully to You. Teach me to wait with patience, hope, and courage.

Help me use this time of waiting to draw closer to You, deepen my trust, and align my heart with Your will. Let every moment of pause become an opportunity to rest in Your presence, listen to Your voice, and grow in faith.

Strengthen my courage and remind me that Your timing is perfect, Your plans are good, and Your love never fails. May I emerge from waiting refined, patient, and rooted in hope.
In Jesus' name, Amen.

Words of Affirmation

- **I wait on the Lord with patience and trust.**
- **God's timing is perfect, and His plans are good.**
- **Waiting strengthens my faith and refines my character.**
- **I release control and rest in God's faithful presence.**

Application: Practicing Waiting Today

1. **Identify areas of your life where you struggle to wait** and consciously surrender them to God in prayer.

2. **Use waiting as an opportunity for prayer and reflection**—even short pauses during the day can become sacred moments.
3. **Journal your thoughts, hopes, and lessons** learned in waiting. Reflect on how God has been faithful in past seasons.
4. **Practice patience intentionally**—remind yourself that waiting is part of spiritual growth, not a delay of blessing.

Waiting transforms our hearts when approached intentionally. It teaches **humility, trust, and reliance on God**, preparing us to embrace His timing and plan with faith and peace.

Closing Reflection

The practice of waiting is a profound spiritual discipline. Through it, we learn to trust God's timing, refine our hearts, and grow in patience and hope. Lent invites us to embrace waiting as a sacred space for transformation and communion with God.

WEEK 4

FASTING & SELF-DENIAL

Theme: Detachment from Worldly Attachments
Scripture Focus: *"But when you fast, anoint your head and wash your face, so that your fasting may not be seen by others but by your Father who is in secret. And your Father who sees in secret will reward you."* — Matthew 6:17-18

Week 4 of our Lenten journey emphasizes **fasting and self-denial**, focusing on detaching from worldly attachments and distractions that hinder spiritual growth. While previous weeks guided us through surrender, repentance, prayer, and reflection, this week challenges us to **intentionally deny the self**, creating space for God to work in our hearts.

Fasting is a spiritual discipline that goes beyond abstaining from food—it can include limiting time on distractions, social media, entertainment, or other comforts that draw our attention away from God. Through self-denial, we learn **discipline, humility, and dependence on God**, recognizing that our ultimate satisfaction comes from Him, not worldly pleasures.

This week encourages:

- **Intentional fasting** — abstaining from something meaningful to deepen focus on God.
- **Self-denial in daily life** — practicing restraint in habits, desires, and attachments.
- **Reflection on God's provision** — acknowledging His sufficiency and faithfulness.
- **Spiritual renewal through simplicity** — detachment from excess fosters a deeper intimacy with God.

By the end of Week 4, the goal is to experience **freedom from worldly distractions, greater spiritual clarity, and a strengthened reliance on God**, preparing our hearts for the final weeks of renewal, surrender, and deepened devotion during Lent.

DAY 22

WHAT ARE YOU HOLDING ON TO?

Theme: Detachment and Surrender Through Fasting & Self-Denial
Scripture Reading:

"Do not love the world or the things in the world. If anyone loves the world, the love of the Father is not in him." — **1 John 2:15 (ESV)**

"And he said to all, 'If anyone would come after me, let him deny himself and take up his cross daily and follow me.'" — **Luke 9:23 (ESV)**

Letting Go to Follow Jesus

As we begin **Week 4 — Fasting & Self-Denial**, today's theme invites you to wrestle honestly with a simple but powerful question: **What are you holding on to?** In a world of abundance, comfort, and constant distraction, our hearts tend to grasp tightly to people, pleasures, habits, or comforts that gradually crowd out our dependence on God. Lent calls us to **detachment from worldly attachments** so that our spiritual senses can be sharpened and our hearts realigned toward God.

Fasting and self-denial are spiritual disciplines that help you *see* what you may not have realized you were clinging to. Whether your attachment is to food, a habit, a desire, or a source of security, denying yourself—even temporarily—reveals the underlying condition of your heart and invites you to surrender what you have held too tightly. Fasting is not an end in itself, but a means of creating space in your life for deeper communion with God.

Reflection: Identifying Your Attachments

Ask yourself these honest questions:

- **What comforts or habits do I reach for when I'm stressed, lonely, or fearful?**
- **What do I depend on instead of God for peace, approval, or security?**
- **Where does my heart turn first when life feels uncertain?**

Fasting helps clarify the answer by *removing the usual sources of satisfaction*. Whether the fast is from food, media, entertainment, or any other habitual distraction, the physical sensation of letting go points you to a deeper spiritual truth: *your soul was made for God.* Instead of merely denying pleasures, fasting helps you recognize the unseen attachments that keep your heart divided.

Consider Jesus' words in Luke 9:23: to follow Him means to **deny yourself and take up your cross daily**. Self-denial is not punishment; it is **redirection**. It turns your attention away from lesser comforts and back toward the One who satisfies every longing of the human heart.

Reflect on these when you notice discomfort during your fast:

- **Am I clinging to comfort instead of trusting God?**
- **Is my identity tied to a habit or approval more than it is to Christ?**
- **Am I holding on to something I need to surrender to God?**

Meditation: Uncovering the Heart's Grip

Find a quiet place and breathe deeply. Close your eyes and place one hand on your heart. Visualize anything that feels heavy, distracting, or habitual that you struggle to release. Let it come into your awareness—not with shame, but with honest sincerity.

Silently pray:

"Lord, show me what I am holding onto. Reveal what competes with You in my heart. I surrender it to You."

Feel the weight of that attachment. Then imagine placing it in God's hands. Breathe in God's presence, breathe out your grip—and let go.

Bible Insight

While fasting during Lent is a traditional way to practice self-denial, its purpose goes beyond abstaining from food; it is about **spiritual clarity and orientation toward God**. Jesus expected His followers to engage in self-denial as a way of disciplining the body and redirecting the spirit toward God's priorities.

Fasting calls us to *feel* what we may have previously ignored—anxiety, restlessness, or longing that points not to God alone, but to something less than God. Once we recognize these attachments, we can consciously place them before the Lord and choose surrender.

Prayer

Loving and Sovereign God,
Today I come before You with an open heart, asking You to reveal what I am holding onto that keeps me from fully depending on You. Show me where my heart is divided.

Help me to see the attachments, habits, comforts, or fears that I have placed above You. Give me courage to surrender them to Your loving care. Teach me to deny myself not out of duty, but out of desire for You—knowing that You alone satisfy every deepest need of my soul.

Transform me through this fast. Let the discomfort reveal where I need Your grace most, and make my heart more like Yours—free, open, and surrendered.
In Jesus' name, Amen.

Words of Affirmation

Speak these truths aloud or silently throughout your day:

- **I release what competes with God for my heart.**
- **My deepest satisfaction is found in Jesus alone.**
- **I surrender my attachments and trust God's provision.**
- **Through self-denial, my spirit grows closer to God.**

Application: Steps Toward Detachment

1. **Name one attachment you sense God leading you to release**—whether food, entertainment, habit, fear, or approval.
2. **Replace that attachment with prayer or Scripture reading** when the urge appears—turn hunger or distraction into communion with God.
3. **Journal your awareness**—what you felt, what surfaces in your heart, and what God reveals.
4. **Offer your fast and denial to God** not as a test of willpower, but as a reminder of your dependence on Him.

Fasting is not merely physical self-denial; it is *spiritual clarity in action*. As you let go of lesser things, your heart becomes freer to hold onto the One who alone satisfies.

Closing Reflection

Fasting and self-denial reveal the unseen places where we cling to comfort, control, or reassurance. Today's invitation is to **notice what you hold tightly and choose to surrender it to God**. In doing so, you participate in a spiritual discipline that deepens dependence, sharpens awareness, and opens your heart to God's renewing work.

DAY 23

FAST FROM FEAR, FEAST ON FAITH

Scripture Reading:

"For God gave us a spirit not of fear but of power and love and self-control." — **2 Timothy 1:7 (ESV)**

"Trust in the Lord with all your heart, and do not lean on your own understanding." — **Proverbs 3:5 (ESV)**

Replacing Fear with Faith

On Day 23 of our Lenten journey, we focus on **fasting from fear and feasting on faith**. Fear can paralyze, distract, and dominate our hearts, limiting our trust in God's goodness and power. Lent calls us to **let go of fear and embrace faith**, reminding us that God's Spirit equips us with courage, love, and self-control.

Fasting from fear is not simply denying worry or anxiety—it is **actively surrendering fear to God**, refusing to let it dictate thoughts, actions, or decisions. Simultaneously, feasting on faith is **choosing trust, obedience, and hope** in God's promises, feeding our spirit with His Word and His presence.

In this season of Lent, practicing this spiritual discipline **strengthens reliance on God, cultivates courage, and transforms fear into spiritual freedom**. Through fasting from fear, we learn that faith is not just belief, but **a lived reality anchored in God's character**.

Reflection: Identifying Fear in Your Life

Ask yourself these reflective questions:

- What fears or anxieties have I been carrying silently?
- How do fear and worry affect my relationship with God and others?
- In what areas of my life can I consciously replace fear with faith?

Fear often masquerades as caution, protection, or concern. Yet Scripture reminds us that God's Spirit brings **power, love, and self-control**—resources far stronger than any fear we face. Recognizing fear is the first step to surrendering it, and intentional faith is the pathway to freedom.

Reflection points:

- **Fear limits obedience**—letting go allows boldness to follow God's leading.
- **Faith strengthens perspective**—trusting God transforms challenges into opportunities for growth.
- **Spiritual nourishment replaces fear**—meditating on God's promises cultivates courage and hope.

Meditation: Feeding Faith

Sit in a quiet place, close your eyes, and breathe deeply. Visualize your fears as dark clouds surrounding your heart. With each exhale, imagine releasing these fears into God's hands. With each inhale, feel faith filling your heart like warm sunlight.

Silently pray:

"Lord, I fast from fear and feast on Your faithfulness. Teach me to trust You in every circumstance and to walk boldly in Your Spirit."

As you meditate, recall times God has been faithful in the past. Let these memories fortify your trust, reinforcing the belief that He is able, loving, and present in every situation.

Prayer

Almighty God,
I confess the fears that bind me and limit my trust in You. Today, I choose to fast from fear—releasing anxiety, doubt, and worry into Your capable hands. Replace them with faith, hope, and courage.

Fill my heart with Your Spirit of power, love, and self-control. Let faith guide my thoughts, words, and actions, transforming every area of my life where fear has taken hold. Teach me to trust Your plans, lean on Your understanding, and walk boldly in obedience to Your will.

Thank You for being my refuge, strength, and ever-present help. May my spirit feast daily on Your promises, drawing courage and joy from Your unfailing love.
In Jesus' name, Amen.

Words of Affirmation

- **I release fear and embrace God's promises.**
- **God's Spirit empowers me with courage, love, and self-control.**
- **Faith strengthens me and guides my daily choices.**
- **I trust God's timing, plan, and provision in all things.**

Application: Replacing Fear with Faith

1. **Identify one fear** you are ready to surrender to God today. Write it down and pray over it.

2. **Feed your faith** with Scripture, reflection, or worship music that reminds you of God's power and love.
3. **Act boldly** in areas where fear has been holding you back, trusting God's guidance.
4. **Journal experiences of faith**—note moments when trust in God replaced fear and how your perspective shifted.

Fasting from fear and feasting on faith is an ongoing spiritual practice. Every time you consciously choose trust over worry, your spirit grows stronger and your heart more attuned to God.

Closing Reflection

Fear diminishes our capacity to live fully in God's presence. By fasting from fear and feasting on faith, we **reclaim spiritual freedom, cultivate courage, and anchor our hearts in God's promises**. Lent calls us to practice this discipline daily, trusting that God's Spirit equips us for every challenge.

DAY 24

LETTING GO OF WORRY

Scripture Reading:

"Do not be anxious about anything, but in everything by prayer and supplication with thanksgiving let your requests be made known to God. And the peace of God, which surpasses all understanding, will guard your hearts and your minds in Christ Jesus." — **Philippians 4:6-7 (ESV)**

"Cast all your anxiety on him because he cares for you." — **1 Peter 5:7 (NRSV)**

The Spiritual Practice of Releasing Worry

On Day 24 of our Lenten journey, we focus on **letting go of worry**—one of the most common ways our hearts become tethered to earthly concerns. Worry can consume energy, cloud judgment, and even strain our relationship with God. Lent invites us to **practice detachment from anxiety**, redirecting our trust to God's care, provision, and timing.

Worry is often a form of subtle self-reliance: when we try to control outcomes or anticipate problems, we forget God's sovereignty and His intimate knowledge of our lives. Letting go of worry is not denying reality; it is **choosing to trust God with outcomes, surrendering control, and resting in His peace**.

Fasting from worry—whether through prayer, reflection, or intentional release—helps us cultivate **inner calm, faith, and spiritual freedom**, freeing space for God to work in our hearts and circumstances.

Reflection: Understanding the Weight of Worry

Consider these reflections:

- **Worry distracts from God's presence**—it shifts focus from faith to fear.
- **Surrender is liberating**—casting anxiety on God brings peace that surpasses human understanding.
- **Prayer is the antidote**—by turning our concerns into requests, we acknowledge God's control.
- **Trust grows with practice**—repeatedly choosing faith over worry strengthens spiritual resilience.

Reflection questions:

- What recurring worries am I carrying that prevent me from fully trusting God?
- How do I typically respond when anxiety rises—do I seek God or rely on myself?
- What would it feel like to release a specific worry to God today?

Philippians 4:6-7 encourages us to **replace anxiety with prayer and thanksgiving**, cultivating a peace that protects our hearts and minds.

Meditation: Releasing Worries

Find a quiet place and breathe deeply. Close your eyes and visualize holding each worry in your hands. One by one, offer them to God, imagining His hands receiving them and transforming them into peace.

Silently pray:

"Lord, I release these worries into Your care. Help me trust Your wisdom, timing, and provision. Fill me with Your peace that surpasses all understanding."

Let the sense of weight lift from your shoulders. Inhale God's calm, exhale fear, and feel your heart lighten as you surrender each concern to His loving care.

Prayer

Gracious God,
I confess the worries and anxieties that weigh heavily on my heart. Too often I rely on my own understanding instead of trusting You. Today, I choose to cast these burdens onto You, confident in Your love and faithfulness.

Replace my anxiety with Your peace. Teach me to pray with thanksgiving, to trust Your timing, and to rest in Your presence. Help me let go of fear, control, and doubt, and to embrace the freedom found in surrendering everything to You.

May Your peace guard my heart and mind, and may I grow in trust, patience, and spiritual strength.
In Jesus' name, Amen.

Words of Affirmation

- **I release worry and trust God with all my concerns.**
- **God's peace surpasses all understanding and guards my heart.**
- **I am not alone; God cares deeply for me.**
- **Surrendering worry strengthens my faith and brings freedom.**

Application: Steps to Let Go of Worry

1. **Identify one worry** dominating your thoughts today and consciously give it to God in prayer.
2. **Write down your worries and prayers** in a journal, physically symbolizing the act of release.
3. **Replace worry with gratitude**—list blessings that remind you of God's faithfulness.
4. **Practice daily surrender**—each time worry arises, pause and redirect your thoughts to God's promises.

Letting go of worry is a **spiritual exercise of trust**, gradually freeing your heart and mind for peace, clarity, and deeper reliance on God.

Closing Reflection

Worry is a natural human response, but Lent calls us to **practice freedom through surrender**. By letting go of worry, we cultivate trust, patience, and spiritual resilience, creating space for God's presence and peace to fill our hearts.

DAY 25

FAST FROM JUDGMENT

Scripture Reading:

"Do not judge, or you too will be judged. For in the same way you judge others, you will be judged, and with the measure you use, it will be measured to you." — **Matthew 7:1-2 (NIV)**

"Therefore encourage one another and build each other up, just as in fact you are doing." — **1 Thessalonians 5:11 (NIV)**

Practicing Compassion Over Criticism

On Day 25 of our Lenten journey, we focus on **fasting from judgment**. Judgment—whether of others or even ourselves—can be a barrier to love, grace, and spiritual growth. Lent invites us to **replace critical thoughts with compassion, empathy, and understanding**, creating space for God's perspective to shape our hearts.

Fasting from judgment does not mean ignoring wrongdoing or avoiding truth. Rather, it is a conscious choice to **pause criticism, extend grace, and seek understanding**. When we fast from judgment, we open our hearts to humility, mercy, and reconciliation, reflecting God's character in our interactions.

This practice encourages us to **look inward**, recognize our own need for grace, and approach others with the same patience and love we hope to receive from God.

Reflection: Recognizing the Spirit of Judgment

Reflection prompts:

- When do I find myself quickly criticizing others or situations?
- How do judgmental thoughts affect my relationships and spiritual growth?
- How can I intentionally replace judgment with compassion today?

Jesus reminds us that **the measure we use for others is the measure used for us** (Matthew 7:2). Our judgments often reveal more about our hearts than about the people we assess. Lent provides a season to **retrain our hearts**, cultivating empathy and understanding instead of condemnation.

Reflection points:

- **Judgment blinds us to God's work** in others' lives.
- **Compassion fosters connection**—building people up instead of tearing them down.
- **Self-awareness is key**—recognizing our own imperfections increases patience and grace toward others.

Meditation: Releasing Judgment

Find a quiet space and sit comfortably. Close your eyes and reflect on moments when you've been critical of others—or yourself. Visualize placing these judgments into God's hands, allowing His grace to transform your heart.

Silently pray:

"Lord, I fast from judgment today. Help me see others through Your eyes and respond with compassion, patience, and love. Teach me to extend the same grace to others that You freely give me."

Let go of any desire to control or condemn. Breathe in God's mercy, exhale criticism, and allow empathy to fill your heart.

Prayer

Gracious God,
I confess the times I have judged others harshly and held critical thoughts in my heart. Forgive me for missing opportunities to show Your love and compassion.

Today, I choose to fast from judgment. Teach me to see others through Your eyes, to respond with understanding, and to build people up instead of tearing them down. Help me extend grace generously, just as You extend it to me.

Transform my thoughts, my words, and my actions so that they reflect Your love and mercy. May my heart become a place of encouragement, acceptance, and reconciliation.
In Jesus' name, Amen.

Words of Affirmation

- **I release judgment and embrace God's perspective.**
- **Compassion and understanding guide my interactions.**
- **I extend grace to others as God extends grace to me.**
- **My words and thoughts build up rather than tear down.**

Application: Practicing Non-Judgment Today

1. **Notice moments of judgment**—pause and ask God for perspective before responding.
2. **Replace critical thoughts with affirmations** about the goodness and potential of others.

3. **Offer encouragement and support** instead of criticism.
4. **Reflect daily** on ways God's grace has transformed your heart and how you can extend that grace to others.

Fasting from judgment is a spiritual discipline that **purifies our hearts, strengthens relationships, and aligns our perspective with God's mercy**.

Closing Reflection

Judgment often hardens the heart and distances us from God and others. By fasting from judgment, we cultivate **humility, compassion, and grace**, opening space for God's love to flow through us. Lent invites us to practice this discipline daily, reflecting Christ's heart in all our interactions.

DAY 26

CHOOSING PATIENCE

Scripture Reading:

"Be still before the Lord and wait patiently for him; do not fret when people succeed in their ways, when they carry out their wicked schemes." — **Psalm 37:7 (NIV)**

"Love is patient, love is kind. It does not envy, it does not boast, it is not proud." — **1 Corinthians 13:4 (NIV)**

The Discipline of Patience

On Day 26 of our Lenten journey, we focus on **choosing patience**—an intentional act of self-denial and spiritual growth. Patience is more than waiting; it is **a posture of trust, surrender, and endurance** in the midst of life's delays, frustrations, and uncertainties.

In a world that values speed and instant results, Lent invites us to slow down, release control, and **allow God to work in His timing**. Choosing patience requires faith that God's plans are perfect and His timing is flawless. It also cultivates inner peace, strengthens relationships, and develops a heart aligned with God's purposes.

Fasting from impulsivity or the desire for immediate gratification creates space for patience to grow. Through self-denial, we learn to endure, trust, and **rejoice in God's timing rather than our own**.

Reflection: Understanding Patience

Reflection prompts:

- In what areas of life do I struggle to wait or endure?
- How does impatience impact my relationship with God and others?
- How can I practice intentional patience today, even in small ways?

Patience is both a fruit of the Spirit and a deliberate choice. By choosing patience, we acknowledge God's sovereignty and demonstrate **trust in His plan, even when circumstances feel slow or difficult**.

Reflection points:

- **Patience demonstrates faith**—trusting God even when outcomes are delayed.
- **Patience fosters compassion**—giving space for others to grow and learn.
- **Patience strengthens perseverance**—enduring trials without complaint or anxiety.

Meditation: Practicing Patience

Sit quietly and take several deep breaths. Reflect on situations where you feel rushed, frustrated, or eager for resolution. Imagine **placing those moments into God's hands**, allowing Him to orchestrate the timing perfectly.

Silently pray:

"Lord, teach me to choose patience. Help me trust Your timing and rest in Your plans, even when life feels delayed or uncertain."

Visualize yourself responding calmly and faithfully in situations that normally test your patience. Let this image guide your heart throughout the day.

Prayer

Faithful God,
I confess my struggles with impatience and my desire for immediate results. Teach me to wait on You with trust, humility, and endurance.

Help me cultivate patience in every aspect of my life—with others, in my work, and in my spiritual journey. May I respond with grace, understanding, and faith, even when circumstances are slow or challenging.

Thank You for Your perfect timing and Your unfailing love. Let patience take root in my heart, shaping my character and deepening my trust in You.
In Jesus' name, Amen.

Words of Affirmation

- **I choose patience and trust God's timing.**
- **God's plans are perfect, even when I do not see them.**
- **Patience strengthens my faith and shapes my character.**
- **I respond to challenges with grace, calm, and trust.**

Application: Practicing Patience Today

1. **Identify one situation** where you feel impatient and consciously surrender it to God.
2. **Pause before reacting**—take a breath, pray, and respond with calmness.
3. **Reflect on God's faithfulness** in past delays or waiting periods.

4. **Journal your experience**—note how intentional patience affects your thoughts, relationships, and peace.

Choosing patience is a daily act of faith that **aligns your heart with God's timing**, strengthens spiritual maturity, and fosters deeper peace in every circumstance.

Closing Reflection

Patience is both a gift and a discipline. By choosing patience, we **surrender control, trust God's timing, and develop endurance** for life's trials and delays. Lent calls us to practice this intentionally, allowing God to cultivate a heart that rests confidently in His wisdom and love.

DAY 27

FAST FROM SELF-RELIANCE

Scripture Reading:

"Trust in the Lord with all your heart, and do not lean on your own understanding. In all your ways acknowledge him, and he will make straight your paths." — **Proverbs 3:5-6 (ESV)**

"Apart from me you can do nothing." — **John 15:5b (NRSV)**

Learning Dependence on God

On Day 27 of our Lenten journey, we focus on **fasting from self-reliance**. Self-reliance often manifests as trying to control outcomes, solve every problem independently, or trust in our own abilities above God's guidance. While competence and diligence are good, overdependence on self can **limit our spiritual growth and cloud our awareness of God's presence**.

Fasting from self-reliance is a spiritual discipline that **teaches humility, trust, and surrender**. By intentionally releasing the need to control or "handle it all" ourselves, we open space for God to work in our hearts, lives, and circumstances. This practice aligns with Lent's broader theme of **letting go of worldly attachments and trusting God fully**.

Through self-denial, we embrace dependence on God's wisdom, timing, and strength. As we learn to rely on Him, our faith deepens, our anxiety diminishes, and our hearts become more attuned to His Spirit.

Reflection: The Cost of Self-Reliance

Ask yourself these questions:

- In what areas of my life do I rely on my own strength rather than God's guidance?
- How does self-reliance affect my prayer life, patience, and trust?
- What would it look like to fully depend on God in my decisions and actions today?

Reflection points:

- **Self-reliance limits God's work**—when we try to do everything alone, we miss opportunities for His provision and direction.
- **Dependence fosters humility**—acknowledging our need for God cultivates a teachable heart.
- **Trust strengthens faith**—relying on God consistently grows spiritual maturity and peace.

John 15:5 reminds us that apart from God, we can accomplish nothing of eternal value. Recognizing this truth is the first step toward **letting go of control and embracing divine partnership**.

Meditation: Surrendering Self-Reliance

Find a quiet place and sit comfortably. Close your eyes and visualize areas where you are relying solely on yourself. Imagine handing them over to God, feeling the weight lift as His wisdom and power take their place.

Silently pray:

"Lord, today I fast from self-reliance. Teach me to depend on You completely, trusting Your guidance, provision, and timing. Help me release control and walk faithfully in Your will."

As you meditate, focus on surrendering both tangible challenges and subtle habits of independence. Feel God's presence reassuring and guiding your heart.

Prayer

Gracious God,
I confess my tendency to rely on my own understanding and strength. Too often I trust my abilities over Your wisdom and fail to recognize my need for You.

Today, I choose to fast from self-reliance. Teach me to depend fully on You, to trust Your guidance, and to surrender control over every area of my life. Strengthen my faith and deepen my humility as I acknowledge Your sovereignty and care.

May my thoughts, words, and actions reflect dependence on You alone, and may Your Spirit guide me in all decisions. Help me walk faithfully in Your ways, knowing that apart from You, I can do nothing of eternal significance.
In Jesus' name, Amen.

Words of Affirmation

- I release self-reliance and trust God's guidance.
- **God's strength is sufficient for every need.**
- **Dependence on God brings freedom and peace.**
- I surrender control and walk faithfully in God's will.

Application: Practicing Dependence Today

1. **Identify one situation** where you are tempted to rely solely on yourself and intentionally hand it over to God in prayer.
2. **Ask for guidance** before making decisions, trusting God's wisdom over your own.

3. **Journal your experiences**—note moments when dependence on God brought clarity, peace, or provision.
4. **Replace self-reliance with prayerful action**—pause before acting impulsively, and invite God into every step.

Fasting from self-reliance trains the heart to **trust God in all things**, cultivating humility, spiritual strength, and a deeper intimacy with Him.

Closing Reflection

Self-reliance is often praised in the world, but Lent calls us to **embrace dependence on God**, acknowledging that His wisdom, power, and love surpass our own. By fasting from self-reliance, we release control, cultivate trust, and invite God to lead every aspect of our lives.

DAY 28

FASTING WITH PURPOSE

Scripture Reading:

"Is not this the kind of fasting I have chosen: to loose the chains of injustice and untie the cords of the yoke, to set the oppressed free and break every yoke?" — **Isaiah 58:6 (NIV)**

"Then Jesus said, 'When you fast, do not look somber as the hypocrites do… But when you fast, anoint your head and wash your face, so that it will not be obvious to others that you are fasting, but only to your Father, who is unseen; and your Father, who sees what is done in secret, will reward you.'" — **Matthew 6:16-18 (NIV)**

Understanding the Purpose of Fasting

On Day 28 of our Lenten journey, we pause to reflect on **fasting with purpose**. Fasting is more than abstaining from food or comfort—it is a **spiritual discipline with intention**, a deliberate act to draw closer to God, gain clarity, and cultivate a heart free from attachments that distract from Him.

Purposeful fasting aligns our physical practice with spiritual intention. It is not performed for show or self-punishment but as a means to:

- Strengthen **dependence on God**
- Cultivate **spiritual clarity and discipline**
- Redirect focus from worldly comforts to **divine priorities**
- Open the heart to **prayer, meditation, and service**

Isaiah 58 reminds us that fasting is deeply relational—it is meant to **transform our hearts and lives**, producing justice, mercy, and compassion alongside personal discipline.

Reflection: Examining Your Fast

Ask yourself:

- What is the intention behind my fast?
- Am I fasting to draw nearer to God or simply denying myself for discipline's sake?
- How can this period of fasting foster spiritual growth and transformation in my life?

Fasting with purpose is an act of surrender. It encourages us to **examine motives**, release superficial practices, and **engage meaningfully with God's Word, prayer, and reflection**.

Reflection points:

- **Fasting purifies priorities**—it helps discern what truly matters.
- **It strengthens spiritual focus**—removing distractions reveals spiritual hunger for God.
- **It empowers intentionality**—every act of self-denial becomes a conscious choice to follow Christ.

Consider how your fasting journey has transformed your heart, heightened awareness of attachments, and deepened reliance on God's guidance. Reflection at this stage of Lent is essential to internalize lessons learned and prepare for continued spiritual growth.

Meditation: Aligning Your Fast with God's Purpose

Sit in a quiet space and reflect on your Lenten fast so far. Visualize the distractions, comforts, and attachments you have let go of. Ask God:

"Lord, show me the purpose of this fast. Teach me to fast with intention, seeking You above all else."

Breathe deeply and imagine each moment of fasting becoming a step closer to God, a spiritual refinement that strengthens your heart and aligns your desires with His will. Allow gratitude for His guidance and discipline to fill your heart.

Prayer

Heavenly Father,
Thank You for guiding me through this season of fasting and self-denial. Help me understand the purpose behind each act of discipline, that it may draw me closer to You and align my heart with Your will.

Teach me to fast with intention, not for appearance or duty, but as a path to deeper communion with You. Strengthen my spirit, refine my priorities, and open my heart to Your presence in every area of life. May this fast produce not only personal growth but also compassion, generosity, and justice in how I live.

I surrender all motives, attachments, and distractions to You. Let my fasting glorify You, and let Your Spirit guide me in every step of this journey.
In Jesus' name, Amen.

Words of Affirmation

- **My fasting is intentional and purposeful, drawing me closer to God.**

- **I surrender all distractions and attachments to God's care.**
- **Every act of self-denial strengthens my faith and spiritual clarity.**
- **I fast with a heart focused on God, compassion, and growth.**

Application: Practicing Purposeful Fasting

1. **Review your fast**—reflect on how it has affected your heart, mind, and spirit.
2. **Identify spiritual lessons**—journal moments of insight, clarity, or transformation.
3. **Connect fasting to action**—consider how your fast can lead to service, prayer, or acts of mercy.
4. **Set intentional goals**—decide how the lessons of this fast can carry forward into daily life beyond Lent.

Purposeful fasting transforms discipline into spiritual growth. It **cultivates clarity, surrender, and deeper communion with God**, ensuring that every sacrifice has meaning and impact.

Closing Reflection

Fasting with purpose is more than abstinence—it is **intentional alignment of heart, mind, and spirit with God**. As Lent progresses, this practice prepares the soul for true renewal, helping us shed distractions, embrace dependence on God, and live with spiritual clarity and intentionality.

WEEK 5

SERVICE & COMPASSION

Theme: Love in Action
Scripture Focus: *Serving others reveals God's heart*

Week 5 of our Lenten journey shifts from personal disciplines to **outward expressions of faith**. This week emphasizes **service and compassion**, highlighting how our spiritual growth is meant to overflow into acts of love, kindness, and generosity toward others.

Jesus modeled a life of selfless service, teaching that **true devotion to God is inseparable from love for others**:

"For I was hungry and you gave me food, I was thirsty and you gave me drink, I was a stranger and you welcomed me..." — **Matthew 25:35 (ESV)**

The purpose of this week is to challenge us to **move beyond our own spiritual journey** and actively live out God's love. Through small or large acts of service—whether offering time, encouragement, or resources—we reflect Christ's heart and demonstrate faith in action.

Reflection questions for the week:

- How can I serve others with humility and love today?
- In what ways does my service reveal God's compassion?
- How can I make love in action a daily habit, not just a seasonal practice?

This week invites intentional practice of empathy, generosity, and care, helping our hearts align with God's desire for justice, mercy, and love in the world.

DAY 29

THE CALL TO SERVE

Scripture Reading:

"For even the Son of Man came not to be served but to serve, and to give his life as a ransom for many." — **Mark 10:45 (ESV)**

"As each has received a gift, use it to serve one another, as good stewards of God's varied grace." — **1 Peter 4:10 (ESV)**

Living a Life of Service

On Day 29 of our Lenten journey, we focus on **the call to serve**. Service is at the heart of Christian living, reflecting the love, humility, and compassion of Christ. Lent is not only a time for personal reflection and spiritual growth it is also a season to **actively extend God's love to others through practical acts of kindness and service**.

Serving is a spiritual discipline that mirrors the example of Jesus, who came **not to be served, but to serve**. It requires humility, intentionality, and a heart attuned to God's guidance. When we serve, we step outside our comfort zones, confront self-centeredness, and align our actions with God's will.

Service is not limited to grand gestures; even small acts of care—listening to a friend, volunteering time, or offering encouragement—reflect God's heart. This Lenten day reminds us that **faith without action is incomplete**, and our spiritual maturity is measured by how we **love and serve others sacrificially**.

Reflection: Understanding the Heart of Service

Reflection questions:

- How do I define service in my daily life?
- What motivates my acts of kindness—love for God or self-recognition?
- Who in my life or community needs my help, encouragement, or presence today?

Key reflections:

1. **Service is an act of obedience** – Jesus commands us to love and serve others, reflecting God's character in tangible ways.

2. **Service develops humility** – In giving of ourselves without expecting reward, we learn to rely on God's grace rather than our own merit.
3. **Service reveals God's heart** – Every act of compassion points others to God and demonstrates His love in action.
4. **Service transforms us and others** – As we extend love outward, our hearts are reshaped, and communities are blessed.

Scripture reminds us that **every believer has unique gifts** meant to serve others (1 Peter 4:10). Identifying and using these gifts is essential for fulfilling God's call to love in action.

Meditation: Preparing the Heart to Serve

Find a quiet place to reflect and breathe deeply. Visualize the people in your life or community who need support, encouragement, or care. Ask God to guide you toward meaningful opportunities to serve.

Silently pray:

"Lord, prepare my heart to serve others as You serve me. Open my eyes to the needs around me and help me respond with humility, love, and compassion. May my actions reflect Your grace and bring glory to Your name."

Focus on releasing any self-interest, pride, or fear that may hinder your willingness to serve. Imagine your hands extended in service, guided by God's Spirit to meet the needs of others.

Prayer

Heavenly Father,
Thank You for the ultimate example of service in Your Son, Jesus Christ. Today, I commit to following His example by serving others with humility, love, and compassion.

Teach me to see the needs around me and respond generously, whether through my time, resources, or encouragement. Remove selfish motives and pride from my heart, replacing them with a genuine desire to reflect Your love.

Lord, let every act of service I perform bring glory to Your name and bless the lives of those I serve. Strengthen me to serve faithfully, even when it is inconvenient or challenging, knowing that in serving others, I am serving You.
In Jesus' name, Amen.

Words of Affirmation

- I am called to serve, and my service reflects God's heart.
- **Humility and love guide my actions toward others.**
- **I use my gifts and abilities to bless and uplift those around me.**

- **Every act of service brings me closer to God and strengthens my faith.**

Application: Practicing Service Today

1. **Identify one person or group** in need of support and take intentional action to help them.
2. **Use your unique gifts**—whether encouragement, listening, teaching, or tangible help—to bless someone today.
3. **Reflect on your motives**—ensure that your service is for God's glory and not personal recognition.
4. **Keep a service journal**—record acts of kindness, noting how serving others impacts your heart and those around you.
5. **Pray for guidance**—ask God to show additional opportunities to serve and love intentionally.

Service is not a one-time act but a lifestyle. By embracing the call to serve, we **extend Christ's love into the world, transform our hearts, and honor God in every interaction**.

Closing Reflection

Serving others is a tangible expression of God's love and an essential part of spiritual growth. Lent challenges us to move beyond introspection, extending the grace, compassion, and generosity we have received. Today, embrace **the call to serve with humility and joy**, trusting that every act of love ripples outward to bless both the giver and the recipient.

DAY 30

COMPASSION FOR THE HURTING

Scripture Reading:

"Finally, all of you, have unity of mind, sympathy, brotherly love, a tender heart, and a humble mind." — **1 Peter 3:8 (ESV)**

"Rejoice with those who rejoice, weep with those who weep." — **Romans 12:15 (ESV)**

Walking with the Hurting

On Day 30 of our Lenten journey, we focus on **compassion for the hurting**. Lent is a season of reflection and renewal, but its ultimate purpose is to cultivate hearts that mirror Christ's love. Compassion calls us to **enter the pain of others, empathize, and act to bring comfort and hope**.

In a world filled with brokenness—whether physical, emotional, relational, or spiritual—Christ calls us to **see, feel, and respond to the suffering around us**. True compassion requires humility, presence, and intentionality. It is not just feeling pity but **engaging in love that heals, supports, and restores**.

Serving those who are hurting is both a privilege and a discipline. It moves us beyond self-centered concerns, transforming our hearts and shaping our lives to reflect the character of Christ.

Reflection: Seeing the Hurting

Ask yourself:

- Who in my life or community is carrying pain, loneliness, or suffering?
- How often do I notice the emotional, physical, or spiritual needs of others?
- In what ways can I respond with empathy, encouragement, and practical help today?

Reflection points:

1. **Compassion requires awareness** — We must first see the needs around us.
2. **Empathy builds connection** — Understanding the struggles of others allows for meaningful support.
3. **Action reflects love** — True compassion is demonstrated through deeds, words, and presence.

4. **Shared vulnerability strengthens faith** — Walking alongside the hurting nurtures humility, patience, and trust in God.

Jesus exemplified compassion throughout His ministry—healing the sick, comforting the mourning, and welcoming the marginalized. As followers of Christ, we are called to **mirror His heart for the hurting in our daily lives**.

Meditation: Opening Your Heart

Find a quiet space to sit in reflection. Close your eyes and picture those around you who are hurting—friends, family, neighbors, or even strangers. Imagine offering them love, comfort, and encouragement.

Silently pray:

"Lord, give me a tender heart that sees and responds to the pain of others. Help me to bring Your comfort, hope, and encouragement to those who are hurting. Teach me to walk alongside them with empathy and humility."

Visualize your hands extended in support, your ears attentive, and your heart fully present, reflecting Christ's compassion to the world.

Prayer

Gracious Father,
I confess the times I have overlooked the pain of others or turned away from their suffering. Forgive me for moments of indifference and teach me to see with Your eyes.

Fill my heart with compassion for the hurting. Help me to respond with empathy, kindness, and practical love. Give me the courage to engage, the wisdom to act appropriately, and the humility to serve without pride.

May my actions bring comfort, hope, and healing, and may Your Spirit guide me in every step of compassion. Let my life reflect Christ's love to those in need.
In Jesus' name, Amen.

Words of Affirmation

- **I have a heart that sees and cares for the hurting.**
- **God's love flows through me to bring comfort and hope.**
- **I am present, attentive, and compassionate toward others.**
- **Acts of empathy and service reflect Christ's heart in my life.**

Application: Practicing Compassion Today

1. **Identify someone hurting**—reach out with a message, call, or act of service.
2. **Listen deeply**—offer your presence without judgment or distraction.
3. **Provide tangible help**—whether emotional support, a kind word, or practical assistance.
    4. **Reflect on the experience**—journal insights about how compassion shaped your heart and the impact it had on others.
    5. **Pray for ongoing sensitivity**—ask God to continually open your eyes and heart to those in need.

Compassion is both a **discipline and a lifestyle**, transforming how we interact with the world and cultivating a heart aligned with God's love.

Closing Reflection

Compassion for the hurting is an essential outgrowth of spiritual growth. Lent reminds us to **look beyond ourselves, enter the pain of others, and extend Christ's love in practical ways**. As we continue our Lenten journey, may we develop hearts that **see, feel, and respond with empathy, service, and humility**, reflecting God's mercy to a hurting world.

DAY 31

ALMS AND KINDNESS

Scripture Reading:

"Do not neglect to do good and to share what you have, for such sacrifices are pleasing to God." — **Hebrews 13:16 (ESV)**

"Give to the one who begs from you, and do not refuse the one who would borrow from you." — **Matthew 5:42 (ESV)**

The Power of Giving

On Day 31 of our Lenten journey, we focus on **alms and kindness**—practical expressions of love and compassion for others. Giving is not just a financial act; it encompasses time, attention, encouragement, and tangible help. Through acts of generosity, we **mirror God's heart and advance His kingdom** on earth.

Lent calls us to **move beyond self-centered living**, fostering a spirit of generosity that blesses others and transforms our own hearts. When we practice alms-giving and intentional acts of kindness, we participate in God's work of restoring hope, meeting needs, and revealing His love in practical ways.

Giving also **teaches humility**, reminding us that all we have comes from God and that we are stewards of His blessings. Through almsgiving, we not only bless others but **draw closer to God**, aligning our lives with His will and purpose.

Reflection: Understanding Generosity

Consider these questions:

- How can I share my resources, time, or gifts to bless others today?
- Do I give out of obligation, expectation, or genuine love?
- How does generosity reflect my trust in God's provision?

Reflection points:

1. **Giving is a spiritual practice**—it expresses faith, gratitude, and obedience to God.
2. **Kindness amplifies generosity**—even small acts of encouragement or help reflect God's love.

3. **Generosity fosters contentment**—releasing what we have helps us recognize God's sufficiency.
4. **Blessing others blesses us**—acts of service and giving cultivate joy, humility, and spiritual growth.

Hebrews 13:16 reminds us that **doing good and sharing what we have are sacrifices pleasing to God**. Each act of giving is a tangible expression of faith and a way to embody the love of Christ.

Meditation: Preparing to Give

Find a quiet space and reflect on the resources, gifts, and time you can offer to others. Imagine extending these as a tangible blessing to someone in need.

Silently pray:

"Lord, teach me to give generously and act kindly. Help me see the needs around me and respond with love, humility, and compassion. May my giving reflect Your heart and bring encouragement, hope, and joy to others."

Visualize your hands reaching out in kindness, your heart open to serve, and your mind attuned to God's guidance in how best to bless others.

Prayer

Gracious God,
Thank You for the many blessings You have entrusted to me. Forgive me for moments of selfishness or neglect, and teach me to give with a joyful heart.

Help me to practice alms and acts of kindness, not out of obligation, but as an expression of love for You and others. Let my generosity meet needs, inspire hope, and demonstrate Your compassion in tangible ways.

Transform my heart to be cheerful in giving, attentive to the hurting, and consistent in acts of kindness. May all I do glorify You and reflect Your love to a world in need.
In Jesus' name, Amen.

Words of Affirmation

- I give generously, trusting God to provide for my needs.
- My acts of kindness reflect Christ's love in the world.
- Generosity blesses others and transforms my heart.
- I am a steward of God's blessings, sharing freely and joyfully.

Application: Practicing Alms and Kindness

1. **Identify one person or group in need**—offer financial help, a meal, or resources if possible.
2. **Perform an act of kindness**—write an encouraging note, make a phone call, or volunteer your time.
3. **Give with intention**—ask God to guide your actions and bless them beyond what you can see.
4. **Reflect on the experience**—journal how giving and kindness impacted both the recipient and your own heart.
5. **Cultivate daily generosity**—look for opportunities each day to bless others in tangible ways.

Through alms and acts of kindness, we **embody Christ's love**, touching lives while growing spiritually and emotionally. Giving is both a discipline and a privilege, reflecting God's generosity in our daily walk.

Closing Reflection

Alms and kindness are powerful expressions of faith in action. Lent invites us to **move outward, bless others, and serve with humility and love**. Each act of generosity, no matter how small, demonstrates God's heart and transforms both giver and receiver.

DAY 32

SHARE YOUR STORY OF GRACE

Scripture Reading:

"But in your hearts honor Christ the Lord as holy, always being prepared to make a defense to anyone who asks you for a reason for the hope that is in you; yet do it with gentleness and respect." — **1 Peter 3:15 (ESV)**

"Go therefore and make disciples of all nations, baptizing them in the name of the Father and of the Son and of the Holy Spirit, teaching them to observe all that I have commanded you." — **Matthew 28:19-20 (ESV)**

Testifying God's Grace

On Day 32 of our Lenten journey, we focus on **sharing your story of grace**. Every believer has a story of God's faithfulness, mercy, and transformative power—moments when His love changed our hearts, provided guidance, or brought restoration.

Sharing our story is an act of **service, witness, and encouragement**. It not only glorifies God but also inspires faith in others, offering hope to those who may be struggling. Lent calls us to reflect inwardly, but it also challenges us to **look outward, proclaiming God's grace through our experiences**.

Your story—no matter how ordinary or humble—can reveal the extraordinary ways God works in lives. By sharing it with humility and authenticity, we **invite others to encounter God's love** while deepening our own appreciation for His transformative power.

Reflection: The Power of Personal Testimony

Ask yourself:

- What are the key moments in my life where God's grace was evident?
- How has God's mercy shaped my decisions, relationships, and perspective?
- Who in my life needs to hear about God's faithfulness and hope today?

Reflection points:

1. **Storytelling is ministry**—sharing your experiences points others to God.
2. **Vulnerability fosters connection**—honest testimony encourages empathy and understanding.

3. **Grace is the message**—highlight God's work, not personal achievements.
4. **Encouragement multiplies**—your story can inspire faith and resilience in others.

Scripture reminds us to **always be ready to give an answer for the hope we have**, doing so with gentleness and respect (1 Peter 3:15). Your story becomes a bridge of faith, offering hope, reassurance, and encouragement to others.

Meditation: Reflecting on Your Grace

Sit quietly and reflect on your journey of faith. Visualize key moments where God's grace guided, comforted, or transformed you. Consider the lessons learned and the ways God's love has been evident even in challenges.

Silently pray:

"Lord, help me to recognize Your work in my life. Give me courage, humility, and wisdom to share my story of grace in a way that honors You and encourages others. May my testimony point others to Your love and faithfulness."

Imagine your story touching hearts, offering hope, and inviting others to experience God's transformative power.

Prayer

Heavenly Father,
Thank You for Your steadfast love and grace in my life. Thank You for moments of mercy, guidance, and transformation that have shaped who I am.

Today, I commit to sharing my story of grace with humility and faith. Help me to speak truthfully, point to Your work, and inspire hope in those who hear it. Remove fear, pride, or hesitation from my heart, and replace it with courage and authenticity.

May my story glorify You, bring encouragement to others, and deepen my own gratitude for Your love. Let my words reflect Your mercy, power, and faithfulness in every circumstance. In Jesus' name, Amen.

Words of Affirmation

- **My story reflects God's grace and power.**
- **I am courageous and humble in sharing my testimony.**
- **Through my experiences, others encounter hope and faith.**
- **God's love shines through my story of transformation.**

Application: Sharing Your Story Today

1. **Reflect on your journey**—identify moments where God's grace was evident.
2. **Choose a platform or person**—share your story with a friend, family member, small group, or through writing.
3. **Focus on God's work**—highlight His mercy, guidance, and transformation rather than personal achievements.
4. **Practice humility and authenticity**—be genuine, vulnerable, and respectful in your storytelling.
5. **Pray for impact**—ask God to use your story to encourage faith, hope, and growth in others.

Sharing your story is a spiritual discipline that **amplifies gratitude, strengthens faith, and blesses others** through the testimony of God's grace.

Closing Reflection

Every believer carries a story of God's love and transformation. Lent reminds us that spiritual growth is not just inward—it is meant to **flow outward, touching lives through acts of service, kindness, and testimony**. By sharing your story of grace, you participate in God's work, inspiring hope and encouraging faith in others.

DAY 33

SEEING CHRIST IN THE OTHER

Scripture Reading:

"Truly I tell you, whatever you did for one of the least of these brothers and sisters of mine, you did for me." — **Matthew 25:40 (NIV)**

"Do nothing out of selfish ambition or vain conceit. Rather, in humility value others above yourselves, not looking to your own interests but each of you to the interests of the others." — **Philippians 2:3-4 (NIV)**

Recognizing Christ in Others

On Day 33 of our Lenten journey, we focus on **seeing Christ in the other**. Every person we encounter—whether a friend, family member, stranger, or even someone difficult—bears the image of God and is worthy of love, respect, and compassion.

Lent is a season of self-examination and spiritual growth, but its culmination is a heart that **extends God's love outward**. Seeing Christ in others challenges us to **move beyond judgment, prejudice, and selfishness**, replacing these tendencies with empathy, patience, and active love.

Jesus' ministry was centered on **valuing the marginalized, listening to the hurting, and responding with compassion**. By training our hearts to see Him in the people around us, we not only serve others but also encounter God Himself in tangible ways.

Reflection: The Lens of Compassion

Ask yourself:

- How do I typically view others—through my biases, expectations, or Christ-like perspective?
- Who in my life might I be overlooking or undervaluing?
- How can I intentionally see and serve Christ in the people I encounter today?

Reflection points:

1. **Every person reflects God's image**—seeing Christ in others reminds us of inherent dignity and worth.
2. **Service becomes sacred**—acts of love are no longer just good deeds but **offerings to Christ Himself**.

3. **Empathy deepens relationships**—recognizing Christ in others fosters understanding, patience, and reconciliation.
4. **Humility transforms perspective**—valuing others above ourselves requires surrendering pride and self-interest.

Matthew 25:40 emphasizes that **how we treat others is ultimately how we honor Christ**. This insight transforms ordinary interactions into spiritual practice and worship.

Meditation: Encountering Christ Daily

Find a quiet place and breathe deeply. Picture the people you will encounter today—neighbors, colleagues, family, or strangers. Visualize **seeing Christ in each of them**, imagining His face reflected in theirs.

Silently pray:

"Lord, help me to see You in others. Open my eyes to recognize Your image and presence in every person I meet. Teach me to respond with love, patience, and humility, seeing beyond my own perspective and serving You through serving them."

Allow your heart to align with Christ's compassion, cultivating a mindset of intentional love and recognition.

Prayer

Heavenly Father,
Thank You for the gift of community and for the opportunity to encounter You in every person I meet. Forgive me for moments when I have judged, ignored, or undervalued others.

Teach me to see Christ in the faces of the people around me. Help me to respond with humility, patience, and love, placing the needs of others above my own desires. May my words, actions, and thoughts reflect Your heart, bringing encouragement, comfort, and hope to those I encounter.

Let me honor You through every interaction, remembering that serving others is serving Christ Himself.
In Jesus' name, Amen.

Words of Affirmation

- **I see Christ in every person I meet.**
- **My words and actions honor God through others.**
- **I respond with humility, love, and compassion.**
- **Every act of service becomes an offering to Christ.**

Application: Practicing Seeing Christ in Others

1. **Pause before interaction**—remind yourself that every person reflects God's image.
2. **Listen actively and empathetically**—seek to understand, not just respond.
3. **Serve with intentionality**—any act of kindness or patience is a service to Christ.
4. **Reflect on encounters**—journal moments where you recognized Christ in others and how it impacted your perspective.
5. **Pray for continued awareness**—ask God to continually open your heart to see Him in everyone you meet.

Seeing Christ in others transforms ordinary interactions into acts of worship, deepening our compassion and aligning our hearts with God's will.

Closing Reflection

Recognizing Christ in others is a profound expression of love, humility, and spiritual maturity. Lent challenges us not only to reflect inwardly but also to **actively see, honor, and serve God through the people around us**. As we continue this journey, let our hearts be trained to perceive His image in every life we touch, cultivating love that mirrors Christ's heart.

DAY 34

THE EUCHARISTIC HEART-GIVE GENEROUSLY

Scripture Reading:

"Each one must give as he has decided in his heart, not reluctantly or under compulsion, for God loves a cheerful giver." — **2 Corinthians 9:7 (ESV)**

"Freely you have received; freely give." — **Matthew 10:8 (ESV)**

Cultivating a Eucharistic Heart

On Day 34 of our Lenten journey, we focus on **the Eucharistic heart**—a heart shaped by gratitude, generosity, and the willingness to give freely, reflecting the grace God has poured into our lives. The word *Eucharist* literally means "thanksgiving," and a Eucharistic heart recognizes that all we have comes from God.

Lent invites us to move beyond self-centered living, teaching us that **true spiritual growth expresses itself in generosity**. Giving generously—whether of time, resources, love, or encouragement is a natural overflow of a heart transformed by God's grace. A Eucharistic heart is marked by **cheerful giving, sacrificial love, and an awareness of God's provision in every circumstance**.

Jesus modeled this through His life, ultimately giving Himself for the salvation of humanity. Following Him means **reflecting His generosity in our own lives**, blessing others not out of obligation but out of a heart overflowing with gratitude and love.

REFLECTION: UNDERSTANDING GENEROUS GIVING

Ask yourself:

- How do I view the blessings in my life—are they possessions, responsibilities, or gifts from God?
- In what ways can I give generously today—of time, resources, encouragement, or love?
- Does my giving reflect gratitude, joy, and trust in God's provision?

Reflection points:

1. **Generosity flows from gratitude** — recognizing God's blessings cultivates a desire to give freely.
2. **Cheerful giving honors God** — acts of generosity are worship when offered willingly, not out of compulsion.
3. **Sacrificial giving reflects Christ** — giving of our time, resources, or talents mirrors Jesus' ultimate sacrifice.
4. **Giving transforms hearts** — generosity shifts focus from self to others, fostering humility, joy, and deeper faith.

2 Corinthians 9:7 reminds us that **God loves a cheerful giver**. Giving from the heart strengthens spiritual maturity, demonstrates trust in God, and blesses both giver and recipient.

Meditation: Opening Your Heart to Give

Find a quiet place and reflect on God's generosity in your life. Visualize the blessings you have received—material, relational, spiritual, or emotional—and imagine offering them back to God in acts of love and service.

Silently pray:

"Lord, teach me to cultivate a Eucharistic heart. Open my eyes to the needs around me and help me give generously with joy, gratitude, and humility. May my giving reflect Your love and provide hope, comfort, and blessing to others."

Picture your generosity flowing naturally, guided by God's Spirit, impacting lives around you, and reflecting His abundant grace.

PRAYER

Gracious Father,
Thank You for the countless blessings You have poured into my life. Forgive me for times when I have held back, been stingy, or given out of obligation rather than love.

Fill me with a Eucharistic heart that recognizes all I have comes from You. Teach me to give generously, cheerfully, and sacrificially, offering my time, resources, and love to bless others. May my acts of generosity point others to Your goodness and draw me closer to You in gratitude and faith.

Let my life reflect Your overflowing grace, and may my giving be a testament of Your love and mercy in action.
In Jesus' name, Amen.

WORDS OF AFFIRMATION

- **I give generously because God has given abundantly to me.**

- My heart overflows with gratitude, guiding my acts of love and service.
- Every gift I share reflects God's mercy and grace.
- Cheerful giving brings joy to others and deepens my faith.

APPLICATION: PRACTICING GENEROUS GIVING TODAY

1. **Identify ways to give**—consider time, resources, encouragement, or acts of service.
2. **Give intentionally and cheerfully**—avoid obligation; let your heart lead.
3. **Reflect on your blessings**—journal moments when God provided abundantly and how that motivates your giving.
4. **Engage in sacrificial acts**—do something that stretches your comfort zone to bless others.
5. **Pray for guidance**—ask God to direct your generosity to those who need it most.

A Eucharistic heart is **a heart tuned to God's provision and love**, extending that love outward through tangible, intentional acts of generosity.

Closing Reflection

Cultivating a Eucharistic heart transforms Lent from a season of self-denial into **a season of joyful giving**. By embracing gratitude, generosity, and sacrificial love, we reflect Christ's heart in our daily lives. Today, let your giving flow freely and cheerfully, honoring God, blessing others, and deepening your own spiritual journey.

DAY 35

REFLECTION-GRACE OVERFLOWING

Scripture Reading:

"But he said to me, 'My grace is sufficient for you, for my power is made perfect in weakness.' Therefore I will boast all the more gladly of my weaknesses, so that the power of Christ may rest upon me." — **2 Corinthians 12:9 (ESV)**

"Every good gift and every perfect gift is from above, coming down from the Father of lights." — **James 1:17 (ESV)**

Experiencing God's Overflowing Grace

On Day 35 of our Lenten journey, we pause to reflect on **grace overflowing** in our lives. Lent is a season of introspection, surrender, and spiritual growth, culminating in the realization that **God's grace is abundant, unearned, and ever-present**. Grace is not only the forgiveness of sins but also the power, presence, and provision of God in every circumstance.

This day invites us to **pause, look back, and see God's work in our journey so far**. From acts of surrender, fasting, prayer, compassion, and generosity, we can recognize the ways His grace has **sustained, transformed, and equipped us** to live intentionally in His love.

Grace overflows when we stop striving to earn it and instead **receive, reflect, and extend it**—to ourselves, to others, and into every aspect of life.

Reflection: Recognizing God's Overflowing Grace

Consider these questions:

- Where have I experienced God's grace in the past 34 days of this Lenten journey?
- In what areas of my life has God's strength been made perfect in my weakness?
- How can I extend the grace I have received to others today?

Reflection points:

1. **Grace sustains in weakness** — God's power is revealed when we rely on Him, not ourselves.

2. **Grace transforms hearts** — His mercy enables us to love, forgive, and serve beyond our natural capacity.
3. **Grace inspires generosity** — Experiencing God's abundance moves us to bless others freely.
4. **Grace invites reflection** — Taking time to notice His work nurtures gratitude, humility, and hope.

2 Corinthians 12:9 reminds us that **God's grace is sufficient**, even when life feels overwhelming, and James 1:17 reinforces that every good gift flows from Him.

Meditation: Reflecting on God's Gifts

Sit quietly and take deep breaths. Reflect on the past weeks—your prayers, sacrifices, acts of service, and moments of surrender. Visualize God's grace flowing into your life, filling every weakness, need, and longing.

Silently pray:

"Lord, I thank You for Your overflowing grace in my life. Help me to recognize Your work in every challenge, blessing, and act of love. Teach me to extend the grace I have received to others, and to live each day with humility, gratitude, and generosity."

Allow yourself to feel God's sustaining presence, acknowledging that His grace is sufficient for every part of your journey.

PRAYER

Gracious Father,
Thank You for Your boundless and overflowing grace. I acknowledge that I cannot earn Your love, nor can I live fully in Your will without Your presence guiding me.

Help me to see Your grace at work in my life—in moments of weakness, in acts of service, in generosity, and in my prayers. Teach me to reflect Your mercy, forgiveness, and love to others.

May the grace I have received overflow into every word, action, and thought, drawing others to You and strengthening my own faith. Let Your power rest upon me, and let my life testify to Your abundant love.
In Jesus' name, Amen.

Words of Affirmation

- **God's grace is sufficient for me in every circumstance.**
- **I am empowered by His mercy to love, serve, and forgive.**
- **Every act of obedience and compassion flows from His grace.**
- **I receive, reflect, and extend God's grace daily.**

Application: Living in Overflowing Grace

1. **Reflect daily**—journal moments where you notice God's grace in your life.
2. **Extend grace**—forgive someone, offer encouragement, or serve without expectation.
3. **Trust in weakness**—lean on God's power instead of relying solely on your own strength.
4. **Celebrate blessings**—recognize every gift, talent, and opportunity as coming from God.
5. **Commit to living graciously**—let your actions, words, and heart reflect God's mercy and abundance.

Grace is not stagnant—it flows outward, transforming lives, nurturing hope, and sustaining spiritual growth. Recognizing and living in God's overflowing grace prepares us to **walk boldly in faith, love, and service**.

Closing Reflection

Lent teaches us surrender, compassion, prayer, and service, but its deepest lesson is that **God's grace is limitless and sufficient**. As we reflect on His abundant mercy, let our hearts overflow with gratitude, humility, and a desire to extend His love to the world.

HOLY WEEK

SUFFERING, DEATH, AND HOPE

Theme: Suffering, Death, and Hope
Scripture Focus: The Passion of Christ

Holy Week is the pinnacle of the Lenten season, commemorating **Jesus' suffering, crucifixion, and ultimate resurrection**. It is a time to reflect on the **depth of Christ's love**, the cost of our redemption, and the hope that emerges from His sacrifice.

This week invites believers to **enter deeply into the Passion**, contemplating the trials, pain, and obedience of Jesus. By meditating on His suffering and death, we are reminded that hope and new life are born through sacrifice and faithfulness.

Holy Week calls us to **walk with Christ in humility, gratitude, and devotion**, preparing our hearts to celebrate the victory of Easter. Scripture reveals that even in the darkest moments, God's purpose unfolds, offering **forgiveness, restoration, and eternal hope**.

Reflection prompts:

- How does Christ's suffering shape my understanding of love and sacrifice?
- Where in my life do I need to surrender and trust God amidst trials?
- How can I live in hope, reflecting Christ's resurrection power to others?

Through Holy Week, we remember that **suffering is never the end**, for Christ's death led to resurrection, and His hope transforms every life that believes in Him.

DAY 36

THE KING OF SURRENDER

Scripture Reading:

"They took palm branches and went out to meet him, shouting, 'Hosanna! Blessed is he who comes in the name of the Lord! Blessed is the king of Israel!'" — **John 12:13 (NIV)**

"For even the Son of Man did not come to be served, but to serve, and to give his life as a ransom for many." — **Mark 10:45 (NIV)**

Recognizing the King of Surrender

On Day 36 of our Lenten journey, we enter **Holy Week** with Palm Sunday, a day that commemorates Jesus' triumphant yet humble entry into Jerusalem. Crowds waved palm branches and hailed Him as King, yet the King they celebrated was unlike any earthly ruler—they were witnessing **the King who surrenders all for love**.

Jesus' kingship is marked not by power, conquest, or self-interest but by **obedience, humility, and surrender to God's will**. He enters Jerusalem knowing the suffering, betrayal, and crucifixion that await Him, yet He **chooses surrender over self-preservation**.

Palm Sunday invites us to reflect on our own lives: **How willing are we to surrender our control, desires, and pride to God?** Like Jesus, true spiritual authority flows from surrender, not domination. His example challenges us to embrace humility, service, and trust even in the face of uncertainty or suffering.

Reflection: Lessons from the King of Surrender

Ask yourself:

- In what areas of my life do I resist surrendering to God?
- How can I follow Christ's example of humility and obedience in daily decisions?
- What does it mean to celebrate a King whose crown is not of gold but of sacrifice?

Reflection points:

1. **Surrender is strength, not weakness** — Christ's obedience demonstrates that yielding to God's plan brings true life and purpose.
2. **Humility precedes exaltation** — The crowds celebrated, but Jesus' true victory comes through the cross. Spiritual growth mirrors this path of humility before God.

3. **Service is central to leadership** — Jesus models a servant heart, teaching that influence and authority are rooted in love and sacrifice.
4. **Faith sustains surrender** — Trusting God's plan enables obedience even when the outcome is unknown or painful.

Mark 10:45 reminds us that Jesus' life and mission were defined by **service and sacrificial love**, not worldly ambition. True surrender invites God to work powerfully through our weaknesses, fears, and limitations.

Meditation: Entering the Palm Sunday Moment

Close your eyes and imagine the streets of Jerusalem. Hear the shouts of "Hosanna!" and see the palm branches waving. Place yourself among the crowd, then imagine walking with Jesus, witnessing His humility and courage.

Silently pray:

"Lord, help me to surrender my pride, fears, and desires to You. Teach me to walk in humility, to serve others selflessly, and to trust Your plan even when it is hard. May I follow the example of Jesus, the King who surrendered all for love."

Visualize yourself laying down your burdens at His feet, offering trust, obedience, and devotion.

Prayer

Heavenly Father,
On this Palm Sunday, I recognize the humility, courage, and surrender of Jesus, my King. Forgive me for moments when I cling to control, resist Your guidance, or prioritize my desires over Yours.

Teach me to follow the King of Surrender in all areas of my life. Give me courage to yield to Your will, humility to serve others, and faith to trust Your plan in times of uncertainty. May my life reflect the obedience, love, and compassion of Christ, drawing others to You through my example.

Let me celebrate Jesus not only with words but with surrendered living, walking in obedience and love each day.
In Jesus' name, Amen

Words of Affirmation

- **I surrender my life to God's will with trust and humility.**
- **My strength grows through obedience and surrender.**
- **I follow Christ by serving others with a humble heart.**
- **The King of Surrender guides my decisions and actions.**

Application: Living Palm Sunday Today

1. **Surrender an area of struggle**—identify a part of your life where you resist God's will and commit it to Him in prayer.
2. **Serve with humility**—perform an act of kindness, volunteer, or help someone without expecting recognition.
3. **Reflect on leadership through service**—consider how humility and surrender can guide your relationships and decisions.
4. **Celebrate the King with worship**—sing, pray, or meditate on Christ's humility, courage, and love.
5. **Journal your surrender**—write down commitments to trust God, noting areas where He is calling you to obedience and faith.

Palm Sunday reminds us that **true victory and spiritual authority emerge from surrender, service, and obedience**, preparing our hearts for the journey to the cross and the joy of resurrection.

Closing Reflection

As we enter Holy Week, Palm Sunday invites us to follow the King who surrenders all. His example challenges us to lay down pride, embrace humility, and serve selflessly. By walking in surrender, we participate in the life, love, and mission of Christ, preparing our hearts to experience the **power of the cross and the hope of resurrection**.

DAY 37

SILENT OBEDIENCE

Scripture Reading:

"And being found in human form, he humbled himself by becoming obedient to the point of death, even death on a cross." — **Philippians 2:8 (ESV)**

"Not my will, but yours, be done." — **Luke 22:42 (NIV)**

The Power of Silent Obedience

On Day 37, we enter **Holy Monday**, a day that emphasizes the quiet, steadfast obedience of Jesus as He prepared for His final week before the cross. Unlike the triumphal joy of Palm Sunday, this day invites us into **reflection, humility, and the often-overlooked power of silent obedience**.

Jesus demonstrated that true obedience is not always loud or public. He fulfilled God's will with **humility, faith, and unwavering dedication**, even knowing the suffering ahead. His silent obedience exemplifies that **faithfulness to God often requires quiet perseverance, surrendering personal comfort and desire for the sake of His greater plan**.

Holy Monday calls us to examine our own lives:

- Are we willing to obey God quietly, even when it is inconvenient, uncomfortable, or unnoticed?
- How can we practice faithfulness in everyday tasks, decisions, and relationships?
- Do we trust God enough to follow His plan without applause, acknowledgment, or immediate reward?

Reflection: Lessons from Silent Obedience

Reflect on these questions:

- What areas of my life require obedience even when no one is watching?
- How do I respond to God's instructions when they conflict with my personal desires?
- Can I embrace humility and trust in God's timing, even in silence?

Reflection points:

1. **Obedience strengthens character** — following God's will in quiet moments builds spiritual resilience and integrity.
2. **Faithfulness is often unseen** — true devotion does not seek recognition but aims to honor God.
3. **Humility precedes impact** — Jesus' silent obedience led to the ultimate salvation of humanity, reminding us that quiet faithfulness carries eternal significance.
4. **Trust is central to obedience** — surrendering our will to God requires faith that His plan is perfect and purposeful.

Philippians 2:8 emphasizes that **obedience may require sacrifice, humility, and even suffering**, yet it aligns us with God's transformative work in the world.

Meditation: Embracing Quiet Faithfulness

Find a quiet space and breathe deeply. Visualize Jesus walking the days leading to the cross, carrying the weight of humanity's sin, yet remaining steadfast in obedience to the Father. Reflect on moments in your own life where God asks obedience quietly—through choices, sacrifices, or acts of service.

Silently pray:

"Lord, teach me to follow You in quiet obedience. Help me to surrender my plans, desires, and will to Yours. Give me faith to trust Your guidance, patience to wait on Your timing, and humility to act faithfully without seeking recognition or reward. May my silent obedience honor You in every area of my life."

Prayer

Heavenly Father,
Thank You for the example of Jesus' silent obedience. Forgive me for moments of defiance, impatience, or self-will. Teach me to obey faithfully, even when it is unseen or challenging.

Help me to surrender my pride and trust in Your perfect plan. Let my actions, words, and decisions reflect quiet faithfulness and devotion to You. Strengthen me to follow Your will with humility, perseverance, and unwavering love, knowing that You see and honor even the smallest acts of obedience.

In Jesus' name, Amen.

Words of Affirmation

- **I obey God quietly and faithfully, trusting His plan.**
- **My silent obedience honors God, even when unnoticed.**
- **Humility guides my actions, and faith sustains my heart.**
- **God's work in my life is fulfilled through faithful obedience.**

Application: Practicing Silent Obedience Today

1. **Identify a small act of obedience**—commit to completing a task, speaking truth, or serving someone without expectation of recognition.
2. **Resist the need for acknowledgment**—focus on pleasing God rather than impressing others.
3. **Journal your reflections**—note ways God leads you to obedience and how it strengthens your faith.
4. **Pray for perseverance**—ask God to help you remain faithful in unseen moments and challenges.
5. **Serve humbly**—find ways to support or bless others quietly, modeling Christ's servant heart.

Silent obedience builds character, nurtures faith, and aligns our hearts with God's will, preparing us for the transformative power of Holy Week.

Closing Reflection

Holy Monday reminds us that **quiet faithfulness and humble obedience** are central to following Christ. Just as Jesus prepared for the cross through steadfast surrender, we are called to trust, obey, and serve faithfully in every season of life. Silent obedience cultivates spiritual depth and aligns our hearts with God's purposes.

DAY 38

TRUTH IN THE FACE OF BETRAYAL

Scripture Reading:

"Jesus answered, 'I have spoken openly to the world. I always taught in synagogues or at the temple, where all the Jews come together. I said nothing in secret.'" — **John 18:20 (NIV)**

"But the Lord said to him, 'Go, show him the truth.'" — **Exodus 18:21 (paraphrased principle for discernment in God's ways)**

Standing Firm in Truth

On Day 38 of our Lenten journey, we reflect on **Holy Tuesday**, a day that highlights Jesus' unwavering commitment to truth amidst deceit, misunderstanding, and impending betrayal. Even as Judas conspired and the religious leaders plotted against Him, Jesus remained faithful to God's Word, speaking truth boldly and without compromise.

Holy Tuesday teaches that **faithfulness to God often requires courage in the face of opposition**. Living in integrity may lead to discomfort, misunderstanding, or even betrayal, but truth grounded in God's Word sustains us and shines light in the darkest circumstances.

This day challenges us to examine our own lives:

- Are we willing to **uphold truth even when it is inconvenient or risky**?
- Do we speak God's Word in love, even when others oppose or misunderstand us?
- How can we remain anchored in faith when betrayal, criticism, or falsehood surrounds us?

Reflection: Lessons from Jesus' Faithfulness

Consider these questions:

- Where have I been tempted to compromise truth for convenience, approval, or self-preservation?
- How can I maintain integrity in speech, actions, and decisions, even under pressure?
- Who in my life needs the witness of Christ's truth through me today?

Reflection points:

1. **Truth requires courage** — speaking God's Word often brings conflict, but it honors Him and aligns our hearts with His purpose.

2. **Faithful witness is countercultural** — Jesus modeled transparency, humility, and love, even when others plotted against Him.
3. **Integrity protects the soul** — living truthfully cultivates inner peace, spiritual clarity, and a strong conscience.
4. **God strengthens the faithful** — in the face of betrayal or misunderstanding, God sustains those who stand firm in His Word.

Jesus' commitment to truth amidst impending betrayal reminds us that **faithfulness is not dependent on external recognition** but on obedience to God's calling.

Meditation: Anchored in God's Truth

Sit in a quiet space and reflect on moments in your life when truth was tested—times of betrayal, misunderstanding, or fear. Imagine Jesus standing boldly in the temple, teaching openly and faithfully, despite knowing the suffering ahead.

Silently pray:

"Lord, give me courage to live in Your truth. Strengthen my heart to remain faithful even when faced with opposition or betrayal. Help me speak with love, act with integrity, and trust that You uphold those who honor You with honesty and faithfulness."

Visualize your life anchored in God's Word, steadfast and unwavering, even in the midst of challenges.

PRAYER

Heavenly Father,
Thank You for the example of Jesus, who faithfully spoke Your truth even when faced with betrayal and opposition. Forgive me for times I have compromised truth for comfort, approval, or fear.

Fill me with courage and integrity to live faithfully in Your Word. Help me to speak truth in love, act justly, and trust You fully in moments of challenge. Let Your Spirit guide my thoughts, words, and actions so that I may honor You, reflect Christ, and shine light in a world that often resists Your ways.

In Jesus' name, Amen.

Words of Affirmation

- **I am anchored in God's truth, even when faced with betrayal.**
- **My words and actions reflect integrity and faithfulness.**
- **Courage and obedience guide me in difficult circumstances.**
- **God strengthens me to stand firm in truth and love.**

Application: Living Truthfully Today

1. **Identify areas of compromise**—reflect on where you may be tempted to avoid truth for comfort.
2. **Commit to honesty**—speak and act in alignment with God's Word, even if it is difficult.
3. **Model faithfulness**—let your life bear witness to integrity and Christ-like obedience.
4. **Pray for courage**—ask God to sustain you in situations where speaking or living truthfully may be challenging.
5. **Reflect on betrayal**—consider how Jesus' example can guide your responses when others oppose or misunderstand you.

Holy Tuesday reminds us that **faithful witness and unwavering truth are acts of courage, love, and obedience**, preparing our hearts to follow Christ all the way to the cross.

Closing Reflection

On Holy Tuesday, we see Jesus as the ultimate model of **truth in the face of betrayal**. His life teaches us that integrity, courage, and obedience to God are worth every challenge, misunderstanding, or opposition. As we continue our Lenten journey, let us **stand firm in God's Word, speak truth in love, and live faithfully even in difficult circumstances**.

DAY 39

RENEWAL IN THE MIDST OF PAIN

Scripture Reading:

"Then one of the Twelve—the one called Judas Iscariot—went to the chief priests and asked, 'What are you willing to give me if I deliver him over to you?'" — **Matthew 26:14-15 (NIV)**

"We also glory in our sufferings, because we know that suffering produces perseverance; perseverance, character; and character, hope." — **Romans 5:3-4 (NIV)**

Finding Renewal in Pain

On Day 39 of our Lenten journey, we enter **Spy Wednesday**, the day that recalls Judas' betrayal of Jesus. It is a day that confronts us with **human weakness, deception, and suffering**, yet simultaneously reveals the **possibility of renewal, hope, and spiritual growth even in the midst of pain**.

Pain is an inevitable part of life. Whether caused by betrayal, personal failure, or circumstances beyond our control, suffering can leave us feeling broken, fearful, or distant from God. However, Scripture reminds us that **pain and struggle are not without purpose**. God uses difficult moments to refine our character, deepen our faith, and open our hearts to His sustaining grace.

Spy Wednesday invites us to **acknowledge the reality of our pain** and to surrender it to God, trusting that He transforms suffering into renewal. Jesus' journey to the cross models this truth: even in betrayal and anguish, He maintained obedience, hope, and love.

Reflection: Lessons from Pain and Renewal

Ask yourself:

- Where in my life have I experienced betrayal, hurt, or suffering?
- How can I surrender my pain to God and allow Him to work renewal in my heart?
- What lessons or growth can emerge from difficult situations?

Reflection points:

1. **Pain can produce perseverance** — difficulties strengthen faith and resilience when met with trust in God.
2. **Suffering cultivates character** — adversity reveals our inner motives and draws us closer to God's purpose.

3. **Renewal emerges from surrender** — yielding our pain to God allows His grace to restore, heal, and empower us.
4. **Hope anchors the soul** — even in betrayal or anguish, hope in Christ sustains and guides us.

Romans 5:3-4 reminds us that suffering is not meaningless; it is a **pathway to spiritual maturity, perseverance, and hope.**

Meditation: Offering Pain to God

Find a quiet place and reflect on any betrayal, failure, or suffering you are carrying. Visualize placing these burdens in God's hands, offering your pain in exchange for His renewal.

Silently pray:

"Lord, I bring my pain, betrayal, and struggles to You. Renew my heart, strengthen my spirit, and guide me through suffering with hope and faith. Teach me to trust Your plan, even when life is difficult, and help me see Your hand transforming pain into perseverance, character, and hope."

Visualize God's light filling the broken places in your heart, restoring, and renewing your spirit.

PRAYER

Gracious Father,
Thank You that You meet me even in the midst of suffering. Forgive me for moments of despair, bitterness, or resistance when faced with pain.

Renew my heart and spirit as I surrender my struggles to You. Teach me to trust that You are at work, transforming trials into growth, despair into hope, and weakness into strength. Help me follow the example of Jesus, who faced betrayal and anguish with obedience, love, and unwavering faith.

May my pain become a pathway for spiritual renewal, and may I emerge from it stronger, humbler, and closer to You.
In Jesus' name, Amen.

Words of Affirmation

- **God renews my heart even in the midst of pain.**
- **Suffering produces perseverance, character, and hope in my life.**
- **I trust God's plan, even in betrayal or difficulty.**
- **My pain is an opportunity for spiritual growth and renewal.**

Application: Experiencing Renewal Today

1. **Identify a painful area of life**—acknowledge betrayal, hurt, or struggle you may have avoided facing.
2. **Surrender it to God**—pray intentionally, asking Him to transform your pain into hope and growth.
3. **Reflect on lessons learned**—journal what God is teaching you through difficulty.
4. **Respond with grace**—seek to forgive, serve, or bless even when you feel wounded.
5. **Anchor in Scripture**—memorize or meditate on verses that remind you of God's sustaining presence in suffering.

Spy Wednesday reminds us that **even the darkest moments can become opportunities for renewal**, teaching us perseverance, character, and hope as we follow Christ toward the cross.

Closing Reflection

Spy Wednesday is a call to recognize that **pain and betrayal are not the end of our story**. God's grace is present, offering renewal, strength, and hope even in the midst of suffering. By surrendering our pain and trusting His plan, we are prepared to experience the transformative power of Holy Week.

DAY 40

LOVE BEYOND MEASURE

Scripture Reading:

"A new command I give you: Love one another. As I have loved you, so you must love one another." — **John 13:34 (NIV)**

"For I have set you an example that you should do as I have done for you." — **John 13:15 (NIV)**

The Depth of Christ's Love

Day 40 marks **Maundy Thursday**, the culmination of our 40-day Lenten journey. On this day, we remember the **Last Supper**, when Jesus washed His disciples' feet and shared the bread and wine, instituting the Eucharist. Maundy Thursday calls us to reflect on **love poured out sacrificially**, humility in service, and the radical nature of Christ's obedience to the Father.

The term *Maundy* comes from the Latin *mandatum*, meaning "commandment," reminding us of Jesus' instruction to **love one another as He has loved us**. His love is unconditional, selfless, and active—**not limited to feelings but expressed through humble action, sacrifice, and service**.

This day invites us to **embrace a love that goes beyond measure**, modeled by Christ's actions in service, sacrifice, and forgiveness. Just as He laid down His life for us, we are called to pour out love in tangible, transformative ways.

Reflection: Living Love Beyond Measure

Ask yourself:

- How does Christ's example of love challenge me to love more fully?
- Are there relationships or communities where I can show sacrificial love today?
- How can I practice humility, service, and forgiveness in my daily life?

Reflection points:

1. **Love is action, not just emotion** — Christ demonstrated love through tangible acts: washing feet, sharing meals, and ultimately dying for humanity.
2. **Humility is essential to love** — serving others requires laying aside pride, personal comfort, and self-interest.

3. **Sacrificial love transforms lives** — even small acts of selfless love have profound spiritual and emotional impact.
4. **Obedience flows from love** — Jesus' obedience to the Father's plan was an act of perfect love for the world.

John 13:34-35 reminds us that **love is the defining mark of a follower of Christ**, and our faith is expressed not only in devotion but in compassionate action.

Meditation: Experiencing and Extending Love

Find a quiet space and imagine the scene of the Last Supper. Picture Jesus kneeling before His disciples, washing their feet, and offering them His love without reservation. Reflect on the ways He has loved you personally and the opportunities He gives you to love others.

Silently pray:

"Lord, teach me to love as You love—selflessly, sacrificially, and without measure. Help me serve those around me with humility, grace, and joy. Show me where my love is needed, and empower me to act boldly, reflecting Your compassion and mercy in every interaction."

Visualize your love flowing outward, impacting your family, friends, community, and even strangers.

Prayer

Gracious Father,
Thank You for the boundless love of Jesus Christ, poured out for me and for all humanity. Forgive me for moments when I withhold love, act selfishly, or fail to serve those in need.

Fill my heart with a love that mirrors Christ—selfless, humble, sacrificial, and unwavering. Help me see every opportunity to serve, forgive, and bless others as an expression of Your love. May my life be a reflection of the love poured out at the Last Supper, drawing others to You through words, deeds, and presence.

Teach me to love beyond measure, obey Your will faithfully, and walk in humility and compassion all my days.
In Jesus' name, Amen.

Words of Affirmation

- **I love others as Christ has loved me—selflessly, sacrificially, and abundantly.**
- **Humility guides my actions, and service defines my faith.**
- **I reflect Christ's love in my words, deeds, and presence.**
- **My life is a vessel of God's boundless grace and mercy.**

Application: Practicing Love Beyond Measure

1. **Serve someone humbly today**—perform an act of kindness without seeking recognition.
2. **Extend forgiveness**—release grudges and show grace to those who have wronged you.
3. **Reflect on sacrificial love**—consider how you can give your time, energy, or resources to bless others.
4. **Celebrate the Eucharist spiritually**—meditate on Christ's gift of Himself and His call to love unconditionally.
5. **Journal your acts of love**—record moments where you chose compassion, humility, or service, noting the impact on you and others.

Maundy Thursday reminds us that **love is the ultimate expression of faith** and the defining mark of Christ's followers.

Closing Reflection

As our 40-day Lenten journey concludes, Maundy Thursday calls us to **live out the love of Christ every day**—a love that surrenders, serves, sacrifices, and forgives. By embracing this love, we not only follow Jesus' example but also participate in His mission of transforming the world.

THE EMPTY TOMB RESURRECTION AND RENEWAL

Scripture Reading:

"He is not here; he has risen, just as he said. Come and see the place where he lay." — **Matthew 28:6 (NIV)**

"Therefore, if anyone is in Christ, the new creation has come: The old has gone, the new is here!" — **2 Corinthians 5:17 (NIV)**

From Surrender to Resurrection

The Lenten journey we have undertaken over the past 40 days is now reaching its glorious culmination: **the resurrection of Jesus Christ**. What began with surrender, repentance, prayer, fasting, and service now culminates in the victory of life over death, light over darkness, and hope over despair.

Easter is not merely a historical event to remember—it is a **present and ongoing reality**. The empty tomb stands as the ultimate symbol that God's grace **transforms lives, restores hearts, and empowers us to live in His divine direction**. Just as Christ rose from the grave, so too are we invited to rise from our old patterns of fear, sin, and self-reliance into a new life of grace, purpose, and freedom.

Reflection: Resurrection as Renewal

Easter is a powerful reminder that **God's work does not end with sacrifice—it begins anew with resurrection**. Consider the transformation that occurs:

1. **Surrender leads to freedom** — our daily acts of surrender are validated and redeemed in Christ's victory.
2. **Pain and sacrifice bear fruit** — struggles, fasts, prayers, and acts of service prepare us to fully experience resurrection life.
3. **Grace is continual** — just as Christ is alive, God's grace is ever-present, renewing us each day.
4. **Divine direction is revealed in the new creation** — resurrection empowers us to walk in purpose, aligned with God's plan.

Take a moment to reflect:

- How has God transformed your heart and life over the past 40 days?
- In what ways can the resurrection inspire hope, courage, and renewed purpose?
- How will you choose grace, mercy, and divine direction as a daily practice?

Meditation: Standing at the Empty Tomb

Imagine approaching the tomb, expecting death and despair, but finding it empty. The stone has been rolled away, and hope stands before you.

Silently pray:

"Lord, I stand before the empty tomb, reminded that You conquer death and redeem all things. Thank You for the grace that sustains me, the love that forgives me, and the purpose that directs me. Help me rise daily into the new life You offer. Teach me to walk in surrender, obedience, and love, and to choose grace in every circumstance. May my life reflect the power of Your resurrection."

Visualize stepping out of the tomb yourself—leaving behind fear, guilt, and doubt, and embracing the **new creation God is shaping in you**.

PRAYER: CHOOSING GRACE EVERY DAY

Heavenly Father,
Thank You for the resurrection of Jesus Christ and the new life it brings. I surrender my old ways, my fears, my failures, and my doubts into Your hands. Renew me each day with Your grace, that I may rise from the old and live as a new creation in You.

Teach me to choose grace daily—in thought, word, and deed. Empower me to follow Your direction, to serve others with love, and to live with faith, hope, and courage. Let the light of the empty tomb guide me, reminding me that nothing can separate me from Your love and that every day is an opportunity to live fully in Your purpose.

In Jesus' name, Amen.

Words of Affirmation

- **I am a new creation in Christ; the old has gone, the new has come.**
- **God's grace renews me every day.**
- **I choose to walk in divine direction, faith, and love.**
- **The resurrection empowers me to live boldly, humbly, and purposefully.**
- **I leave fear, doubt, and guilt behind and embrace hope, freedom, and life in Christ.**

APPLICATION: LIVING RESURRECTION LIFE

1. **Daily Renewal:** Begin each morning by consciously choosing to live in grace, surrender, and obedience. Reflect on one way you can embody Christ's resurrection life that day.
2. **Spiritual Direction:** Set aside intentional time for prayer, Scripture meditation, and journaling to discern God's guidance.

3. **Acts of Love:** Let your life overflow with compassion, service, and generosity, reflecting Christ's sacrificial love.
4. **Letting Go:** Release old habits, resentment, or fears that hinder your walk with God. Step into freedom through His resurrection power.
5. **Community and Witness:** Share the hope and renewal of Christ with others through encouragement, mentoring, or volunteering.

Epilogue: Choosing Grace Every Day

Resurrection is not a one-time event; it is **an ongoing invitation to live in divine love, surrender, and purpose**. The empty tomb reminds us that God's grace is relentless, His mercy is abundant, and His direction is perfect.

Choosing grace every day means:

- **Trusting God's plan** even when the path is unclear.
- **Serving others with humility and compassion.**
- **Forgiving freely** as you have been forgiven.
- **Living courageously** in obedience to God's Word.
- **Sharing hope** through words, deeds, and witness.

Let the lessons of Lent—surrender, repentance, prayer, fasting, service, and reflection—guide your daily walk in the power of Christ's resurrection.

Appendices

Appendix A: Daily Scripture Index

A list of all 40 Scripture passages used in the devotional, organized by day for easy reference.

Appendix B: Prayer and Reflection Templates

Templates for journaling reflections, prayer prompts, and areas of surrender, forgiveness, and gratitude.

Appendix C: Lent Checklist

A practical checklist for daily surrender, meditation, fasting, service, and Scripture reading to continue spiritual growth beyond Lent.

Appendix D: Suggested Resources

- Recommended books, devotionals, and online resources for further study of Lent, Holy Week, and Christian discipleship.
- Scripture memory verses for meditation and reinforcement of themes.

Appendix E: Personal Reflection Journal Pages

Blank or guided pages for the reader to continue recording insights, answered prayers, and moments of grace beyond the 40-day journey.

Fin al Thoughts

Surrendered Grace is not just a 40-day journey—it is a lifelong practice. Easter reminds us that **God's work does not end in sacrifice alone**; it continues in resurrection, renewal, and purpose. Every day offers a choice: to live in fear or faith, in old habits or new life, in self-reliance or surrendered grace.

As you step forward, remember:

- The empty tomb empowers you to live boldly.
- Grace is your constant companion.
- Divine direction is available as you seek God with a surrendered heart.
- Love and service are the evidence of resurrection life in action.

Carry these truths with you, and let **every day be a celebration of God's grace, mercy, and transformative love**.

SCRIPTURE INDEX - 40 DAYS OF LENT

Week 1 — Surrender

Theme: Letting Go for Renewal

- **Day 1: Ash Wednesday — A Call to Surrender**
  Joel 2:12-13; Psalm 51:10; Matthew 6:33
- **Day 2: Dust and Grace — Acknowledging Human Frailty**
  Genesis 3:19; Psalm 103:14; 2 Corinthians 12:9
- **Day 3: Confession of the Heart**
  1 John 1:9; Psalm 32:5; Proverbs 28:13
- **Day 4: Facing the Wilderness Within**
  Matthew 4:1-11; Isaiah 43:2; Psalm 23:4
- **Day 5: Surrendering Control**
  Proverbs 3:5-6; Philippians 4:6-7; Romans 12:1
- **Day 6: Choosing Obedience**
  John 14:15; Hebrews 5:8; James 1:22
- **Day 7: Rest Day Reflection — Sabbath in the Middle of Lent**
  Exodus 20:8-11; Matthew 11:28-30; Psalm 46:10

Week 2 — Repentance & Forgiveness

Theme: Turning Back to God

- **Day 8: Turning from Sin**
  Acts 3:19; Isaiah 55:7; Psalm 51:17
- **Day 9: The Gift of Forgiveness**
  Ephesians 1:7; Colossians 3:13; Matthew 6:14-15
- **Day 10: Grace That Cleanses**
  Titus 2:11-12; 1 Peter 1:22; Hebrews 10:22
- **Day 11: Renewal of the Mind**
  Romans 12:2; Ephesians 4:23; Philippians 4:8
- **Day 12: Repairing Broken Relationships**
  Matthew 5:23-24; Proverbs 16:7; Romans 15:5-6
- **Day 13: Extending Forgiveness to Others**
  Luke 6:37; Matthew 18:21-22; Colossians 3:13
- **Day 14: Reflection, The Freedom of Forgiveness**
  Psalm 103:12; Isaiah 1:18; 2 Corinthians 5:18

Week 3 — Prayer and Contemplation

Theme: Deepening Communion with God

- **Day 15: Silence and Solitude**
  Mark 1:35; Psalm 46:10; Luke 5:16

- **Day 16: Praying Without Ceasing**
  1 Thessalonians 5:16-18; Romans 12:12; Philippians 4:6
- **Day 17: Listening for God's Voice**
  John 10:27; Psalm 119:105; Isaiah 30:21
- **Day 18: Petition — Asking, Seeking, Knock**
  Matthew 7:7-8; James 4:2; Philippians 4:19
- **Day 19: Gratitude Through the Storm**
  1 Thessalonians 5:18; Psalm 107:28-31; Colossians 3:15-17
- **Day 20: Adoration — Worship in Truth**
  John 4:23-24; Psalm 95:6-7; Hebrews 13:15
- **Day 21: Reflection, The Practice of Waiting**
  Isaiah 40:31; Psalm 27:14; Lamentations 3:25-26

Week 4 — Fasting & Self-Denial

Theme: Detachment from Worldly Attachments

- **Day 22: What Are You Holding On To?**
  Matthew 6:19-21; Luke 14:33; James 4:7
- **Day 23: Fast from Fear, Feast on Faith**
  2 Timothy 1:7; Psalm 56:3; Isaiah 41:10
- **Day 24: Letting Go of Worry**
  Matthew 6:25-34; Philippians 4:6-7; 1 Peter 5:7
- **Day 25: Fast from Judgment**
  Matthew 7:1-5; Romans 14:13; James 4:11
- **Day 26: Choosing Patience**
  Romans 8:25; Galatians 5:22; Psalm 37:7
- **Day 27: Fast from Self-Reliance**
  Proverbs 3:5-6; John 15:5; Isaiah 30:15
- **Day 28: Reflection, Fasting with Purpose**
  Matthew 4:1-4; Isaiah 58:6-11; Joel 2:12-13

Week 5 — Service & Compassion

Theme: Love in Action

- **Day 29: The Call to Serve**
  Mark 10:45; John 13:12-15; Galatians 5:13
- **Day 30: Compassion for the Hurting**
  Colossians 3:12; Matthew 25:34-36; Isaiah 61:1
- **Day 31: Alms and Kindness**
  Proverbs 19:17; Luke 6:38; Acts 20:35
- **Day 32: Share Your Story of Grace**
  Psalm 107:2; Revelation 12:11; 1 Peter 3:15
- **Day 33: Seeing Christ in the Other**
  Matthew 25:40; John 1:14; 1 John 4:20-21
- **Day 34: The Eucharistic Heart — Give Generously**
  Luke 22:19-20; 2 Corinthians 9:7; John 6:35
- **Day 35: Reflection, Grace Overflowing**
  Romans 5:5; Ephesians 3:16-19; 2 Corinthians 1:3-4

Holy Week — Suffering, Death, and Hope

- **Day 36: Palm Sunday — The King of Surrender**
  John 12:12-13; Mark 10:45; Zechariah 9:9
- **Day 37: Holy Monday — Silent Obedience**
  Philippians 2:8; Luke 22:42; Hebrews 5:8
- **Day 38: Holy Tuesday — Truth in the Face of Betrayal**
  John 18:20; Exodus 18:21 (principle); Matthew 26:3-5
- **Day 39: Spy Wednesday — Renewal in the Midst of Pain**
  Matthew 26:14-15; Romans 5:3-4; 2 Corinthians 4:16-18
- **DAY 40: Maundy Thursday — Love Beyond Measure**
  John 13:34-35; John 13:15; 1 John 4:7-8

Appendices (Scripture Cross-Reference)

- **Forgiveness & Repentance:** Psalm 32, Isaiah 55, 1 John 1:9
- **Prayer & Contemplation:** Matthew 6:6, Luke 5:16, Philippians 4:6-7
- **Fasting & Self-Denial:** Isaiah 58:6-11, Matthew 4:1-4, Luke 14:33
- **Service & Compassion:** Matthew 25:34-40, Galatians 5:13, 1 Peter 3:15
- **Holy Week & Resurrection:** John 12-21, Matthew 26-28, Luke 22-2

FINAL WORD

LIVING OUT SURRENDERED GRACE

As your 40-day journey draws to a close, take a moment to **reflect on the spiritual transformation you've experienced**. The journey of Lent is not only about **personal discipline** but about **deepening your surrender to God**, embracing His grace, and aligning your life with His divine direction.

Reflections on the Journey

1. **Surrender Deepens Spiritual Resilience:**
   Each act of surrender—confession, fasting, prayer, or service—teaches us to **release control** and trust God's perfect plan. Surrender is not weakness; it is the **strength to follow God despite uncertainty**.
2. **Grace Renews Daily:**
   Lent reminds us that grace is **continuous and transformative**. Each morning offers a chance to start anew, forgiving ourselves and others, and walking in renewed freedom and hope.
3. **Divine Direction Becomes Clearer:**
   When the heart is surrendered, God's guidance becomes **more perceptible in prayer, Scripture, and reflection**. The journey helps you discern His will, make choices aligned with His purposes, and respond faithfully to the needs around you.
4. **Love in Action Transforms Lives:**
   Through acts of service, compassion, and generosity, God's grace flows through you to impact others. What began as an inward journey of surrender now **expands outward**, leaving tangible marks of His love in your world.

PRACTICAL STEPS TO CONTINUE LIVING SURRENDERED GRACE

- **Daily Surrender:** Begin each day by consciously offering your plans, thoughts, and actions to God.
- **Ongoing Prayer & Reflection:** Keep a journal or devotion time to maintain a dialogue with God.
- **Service & Compassion:** Continue acts of kindness, intentional listening, and generosity.
- **Scripture Meditation:** Regularly engage with God's Word to align your heart with His direction.
- **Celebrate Grace:** Remember God's faithfulness and reflect on answered prayers, small or large.

Final Encouragement

Your journey through Lent has been a **practice in surrender, reflection, and renewal**. The lessons learn letting go of control, embracing repentance, deepening prayer life, fasting with purpose, serving others, and walking with Christ in Holy Week are **not limited to 40 days**.

Living out **Surrendered Grace** means:

- Trusting God even when the path is unclear.
- Choosing forgiveness over bitterness.
- Practicing humility and service in daily interactions.
- Walking intentionally in the light of Christ's resurrection.
- Allowing God's love to guide your decisions, actions, and relationships.

As you continue beyond this devotional, remember that **every day is an opportunity to choose grace, surrender, and divine direction**. May your heart remain open, your hands ready to serve, and your life a reflection of the boundless love of Christ.

Manufactured by Amazon.ca
Bolton, ON